# www.EffortlessMath.com

... So Much More Online!

✓ FREE Math lessons

✓ More Math learning books!

✓ Mathematics Worksheets

✓ Online Math Tutors

**Need a PDF version of this book?**

Please visit www.EffortlessMath.com

# 5 Full-Length STAAR Grade 8 Math Practice Tests

*The Practice You Need to Ace the STAAR*

*Math Test*

By

Reza Nazari & Ava Ross

All inquiries should be addressed to:

info@effortlessMath.com

www.EffortlessMath.com

**ISBN-13:** 978-1-970036-60-2

**ISBN-10:** 1-970036-60-5

**Published by: Effortless Math Education**

**www.EffortlessMath.com**

# Description

**5 Full-Length STAAR Grade 8 Math Practice Tests**, which reflects the 2020 test guidelines and topics, is designed to help you hone your math skills, overcome your exam anxiety, and boost your confidence -- and do your best to ace the STAAR Math Test. The realistic and full-length STAAR Math tests, which reflect the format and question types on the STAAR, show you how the test is structured and what math topics you need to master. The practice test questions are followed by answer explanations to help you find your weak areas, learn from your mistakes, and raise your STAAR Math score.

The surest way to succeed on STAAR Math Test is with intensive practice in every math topic tested-- and that's what you will get in **5 Full-Length STAAR Grade 8 Math Practice Tests**. This STAAR Math new edition has been updated to replicate questions appearing on the most recent STAAR Math tests. This is a precious learning tool for STAAR Math test takers who need extra practice in math to improve their STAAR Math score. After taking the STAAR Math practice tests in this book, you will have solid foundation and adequate practice that is necessary to succeed on the STAAR Grade 8 Math test. **This book is your ticket to ace the STAAR Math Test!**

**5 Full-Length STAAR Grade 8 Math Practice Tests** contains many exciting and unique features to help you improve your test scores, including:

- Content 100% aligned with the 2020 STAAR test

- Written by STAAR Math tutors and test experts

- Complete coverage of all STAAR Math concepts and topics which you will be tested

- Detailed answers and explanations for every STAAR Math practice questions to help you learn from your mistakes

- 5 full-length practice tests (featuring new question types) with detailed answers

This STAAR Math book and other Effortless Math Education books are used by thousands of students each year to help them review core content areas, brush-up in math, discover their strengths and weaknesses, and achieve their best scores on the STAAR test.

## About the Author

**Reza Nazari** is the author of more than 100 Math learning books including:
– **Math and Critical Thinking Challenges:** For the Middle and High School Student
– **STAAR Math in 30 Days**
– **ASVAB Math Workbook 2018 - 2019**
– **Effortless Math Education Workbooks**
– **and many more Mathematics books …**

Reza is also an experienced Math instructor and a test–prep expert who has been tutoring students since 2008. Reza is the founder of Effortless Math Education, a tutoring company that has helped many students raise their standardized test scores—and attend the colleges of their dreams. Reza provides an individualized custom learning plan and the personalized attention that makes a difference in how students view math.

You can contact Reza via email at:
reza@EffortlessMath.com

Find Reza's professional profile at:
goo.gl/zoC9rJ

# Contents

# STAAR Test Review

The State of Texas Assessments of Academic Readiness (STAAR) is developed under the supervision of the Texas Education Agency and is taken by all public school students in Texas, grades 3–12. The tests measure the progress of students from $3^{rd}$ grade to $8^{th}$ grade, as well as high school. STAAR is the state's testing program and is based on state curriculum standards in core subjects including:

- o Reading,
- o Writing,
- o Mathematics,
- o Science,
- o Social Studies

In high school, students take end-of-course STAAR exams in five high school subjects:

- o Algebra I,
- o Biology,
- o English I,
- o English II,
- o U.S. History.

Students take STAAR tests in the spring. The number of tests a student takes each year will depend on what grade he or she is in. Most students will have two to four testing days during a school year.

In this book, there are five complete Grade 8 STAAR Math Tests. Take these tests to see what score you'll be able to receive on a real STAAR Math test.

Good luck!

## Time to refine your skill with a practice examination

Take a practice STAAR Math Test to simulate the test day experience. After you've finished, score your test using the answer key.

## Before You Start

- You'll need a pencil and a calculator to take the test.

- There are two types of questions:

  Multiple choice questions: for each of these questions, there are four or more possible answers. Choose which one is best.

  Grid-ins questions: for these questions, write your answer in the box provided.

- It's okay to guess. You won't lose any points if you're wrong.

- The STAAR Mathematics test contains a formula sheet, which displays formulas relating to geometric measurement and certain algebra concepts. Formulas are provided to test-takers so that they may focus on application, rather than the memorization, of formulas.

- After you've finished the test, review the answer key to see where you went wrong and what areas you need to improve.

**Good luck!**

# STAAR Mathematics Practice Test 1

## 2020

**Grade 8**

**Total number of questions:** 40

**Total time to complete the test:** No time limit

**You may use a calculator on this practice test.**

# STAAR Grade 8 Mathematics Formula Sheet

## LINEAR EQUATIONS

| | |
|---|---|
| **Slope – intercept form** | $y = mx + b$ |
| **Direct Variation** | $y = kx$ |
| **Slope of a Line** | $m = \dfrac{y_2 - y_1}{x_2 - x_1}$ |

## CIRCUMFERENCE

| | |
|---|---|
| **Circle** | $C = 2\pi r$ or $C = \pi d$ |

## AREA

| | |
|---|---|
| Triangle | $A = \dfrac{1}{2}bh$ |
| Parallelogram | $A = bh$ |
| Trapezoid | $A = \dfrac{1}{2}h(b_1 + b_2)$ |
| Circle | $A = \pi r^2$ |

## SURFACE AREA

| | Lateral | Total |
|---|---|---|
| Prism | $S = Ph$ | $S = Ph + 2B$ |
| Cylinder | $S = 2\pi rh$ | $S = 2\pi rh + 2\pi r^2$ |

## VOLUME

| | |
|---|---|
| Prism or Cylinder | $V = Bh$ |
| Pyramid or Cone | $V = \dfrac{1}{3}Bh$ |
| Sphere | $V = \dfrac{4}{3}\pi r^3$ |

## ADDITIONAL INFORMATION

| | |
|---|---|
| Pythagorean theorem | $a^2 + b^2 = c^2$ |
| Simple interest | $I = prt$ |
| Compound Interest | $A = p(1 + r)^t$ |

1) In the rectangle below if $y > 5$ cm and the area of rectangle is 50 cm2 and the perimeter of the rectangle is 30 cm, what is the value of $x$ and $y$ respectively?
   - ☐A. 4, 11
   - ☐B. 5, 11
   - ☐C. 5, 10
   - ☐D. 4, 10

2) What is the length of AB in the following figure if AE = 4, CD = 6 and AC = 12?

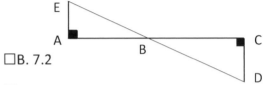

   - ☐A. 3.8
   - ☐B. 7.2
   - ☐C. 4.8
   - ☐D. 24

3) If a gas tank can hold 25 gallons, how many gallons does it contain when it is $\frac{2}{5}$ full?
   - ☐A. 50
   - ☐B. 62.5
   - ☐C. 125
   - ☐D. 10

4) What is the area of the shaded region?
   - ☐A. 31 $ft$
   - ☐B. 64 $ft$
   - ☐C. 40 $ft$
   - ☐D. 80 $ft$

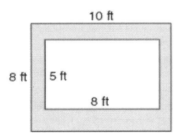

5) What is the value of this expression? $[3 \times (-14) - 48] - (-14) + [3 \times 8] \div 2$

   Write your answer in the box below.

   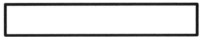

6) What is the product of all possible values of $x$ in the following equation?

$$|2x - 6| = 12$$

   - ☐A. −27
   - ☐B. −3
   - ☐C. 9
   - ☐D. 27

7) What is the slope of a line that is perpendicular to the line $3x - y = 6$?

☐A. $-3$ ☐B. $-\frac{1}{3}$

☐C. $2$ ☐D. $6$

8) What is the value of the expression $3(x - 2y) + (2 - x)^2$ when $x = 5$ and $y = -3$ ?

☐A. $-22$ ☐B. $24$

☐C. $42$ ☐D. $88$

9) If $x - 4(x + 2) = -15.5$, what is the value of $x$?

Write your answer in the box below.

10) Which of the following answers represents the compound inequality $-4 \leq 4x - 8 < 16$?

☐A. $-2 \leq x \leq 8$ ☐B. $-2 < x \leq 8$
☐C. $1 < x \leq 6$ ☐D. $1 \leq x < 6$

11) Simplify the expression.

$$(6x^3 - 8x^2 + 2x^4) - (4x^2 - 2x^4 + 2x^3)$$

☐A. $4x^4 + 4x^3 - 12x^2$ ☐B. $4x^3 - 12x^2$

☐C. $4x^4 + 4x^3 + 12x^2$ ☐D. $8x^3 - 12x^2$

12) In two successive years, the population of a town is increased by 15% and 20%. What percent of the population is increased after two years?

☐A. 32% ☐B. 35%

☐C. 38% ☐D. 68%

13) Last week 24,000 fans attended a football match. This week three times as many bought tickets, but one sixth of them cancelled their tickets. How many are attending this week?

☐A. 48,000                           ☐B. 54,000

☐C. 60,000                          ☐D. 72,000

14) What is the perimeter of a square in centimeters that has an area of $595.36\ cm^2$?

Write your answer in the box below. (don't write the measurement)

15) The mean of 50 test scores was calculated as 88. But, it turned out that one of the scores was misread as 94 but it was 69. What is the correct mean of the test scores?

☐A. 85                                ☐B. 87

☐C. 87.5                            ☐D. 88.5

16) Two dice are thrown simultaneously, what is the probability of getting a sum of 5 or 8?

☐A. $\dfrac{1}{3}$                            ☐B. $\dfrac{1}{4}$

☐C. $\dfrac{1}{16}$                         ☐D. $\dfrac{11}{36}$

17) A swimming pool holds 2,000 cubic feet of water. The swimming pool is 25 feet long and 10 feet wide. How deep is the swimming pool?

Write your answer in the box below. (<u>Don't write the measurement</u>)

18) Mr. Carlos family are choosing a menu for their reception. They have 3 choices of appetizers, 5 choices of entrees, 4 choices of cake. How many different menu combinations are possible for them to choose?

☐A. 12                               ☐B. 32

☐C. 60                               ☐D. 120

19) In a stadium the ratio of home fans to visiting fans in a crowd is $5:7$. Which of the following could be the total number of fans in the stadium?

☐A. 12,324                    ☐C. 44,566

☐B. 42,326                    ☐D. 66,812

20) What is the area of a square whose diagonal is 8?

☐A. 16                    ☐B. 32

☐C. 36                    ☐D. 64

21) Anita's trick–or–treat bag contains 12 pieces of chocolate, 18 suckers, 18 pieces of gum, 24 pieces of licorice. If she randomly pulls a piece of candy from her bag, what is the probability of her pulling out a piece of sucker?

☐A. $\frac{1}{3}$                    ☐B. $\frac{1}{4}$

☐C. $\frac{1}{6}$                    ☐D. $\frac{1}{12}$

22) The perimeter of a rectangular yard is 60 meters. What is its length if its width is twice its length?

☐A. 10 meters                    ☐B. 18 meters

☐C. 20 meters                    ☐D. 24 meters

23) The average of 6 numbers is 12. The average of 4 of those numbers is 10. What is the average of the other two numbers.

☐A. 10                    ☐B. 12

☐C. 14                    ☐D. 16

24) What is the value of $x$ in the following system of equations?

$$2x + 5y = 11$$
$$4x - 2y = -14$$

☐A. $-1$                    ☐B. 1

☐C. $-2$                    ☐D. 4

25) The perimeter of the trapezoid below is 36 *cm*. What is its area?

□A. 576 $cm^2$        □B. 70 $cm^2$

□C. 48 $cm^2$         □D. 24 $cm^2$

12 *cm*

6 *cm*            8 *cm*

26) A card is drawn at random from a standard 52–card deck, what is the probability that the card is of Hearts? (The deck includes 13 of each suit clubs, diamonds, hearts, and spades)

□A. $\dfrac{1}{3}$        □B. $\dfrac{1}{4}$

□C. $\dfrac{1}{6}$        □D. $\dfrac{1}{52}$

27) The average of five numbers is 25. If a sixth number that is greater than 42 is added, then, which of the following could be the new average?

□A. 25        □C. 27

□B. 26        □D. 28

28) The diagonal of a rectangle is 10 inches long and the height of the rectangle is 8 inches. What is the perimeter of the rectangle in inches?

Write your answer in the box below.

29) The ratio of boys and girls in a class is 4: 7. If there are 44 students in the class, how many more boys should be enrolled to make the ratio 1: 1?

□A. 8        □B. 10

□C. 12       □D. 14

30) Mr. Jones saves $2,500 out of his monthly family income of $55,000. What fractional part of his income does he save?

□A. $\dfrac{1}{22}$        □B. $\dfrac{1}{11}$

□C. $\dfrac{3}{25}$        □D. $\dfrac{2}{15}$

31) Jason needs an 75% average in his writing class to pass. On his first 4 exams, he earned scores of 68%, 72%, 85%, and 90%. What is the minimum score Jason can earn on his fifth and final test to pass?

Write your answer in the box below.

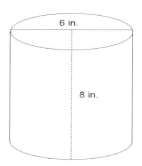

32) What is the value of $x$ in the following equation? $\frac{2}{3}x + \frac{1}{6} = \frac{1}{3}$

☐A. 6          ☐B. $\frac{1}{2}$

☐C. $\frac{1}{3}$          ☐D. $\frac{1}{4}$

33) A bank is offering 3.5% simple interest on a savings account. If you deposit $12,000, how much interest will you earn in two years?

☐A. $420          ☐B. $840

☐C. $4200         ☐D. $8,400

34) Simplify $6x^2y^3(2x^2y)^3 =$

☐A. $12x^4y^6$        ☐B. $12x^8y^6$

☐C. $48x^4y^6$        ☐D. $48x^8y^6$

35) What is the surface area of the cylinder below?

☐A. $48\,\pi\,in^2$        ☐B. $57\,\pi\,in^2$

☐C. $66\,\pi\,in^2$        ☐D. $288\,\pi\,in^2$

36) A cruise line ship left Port $A$ and traveled 80 miles due west and then 150 miles due north. At this point, what is the shortest distance from the cruise to port $A$ in miles?

Write your answer in the box below.

37) What is the equivalent temperature of $104°F$ in Celsius? $C = \frac{5}{9}(F - 32)$

☐A. 32 ☐B. 40

☐C. 48 ☐D. 52

38) The circle graph below shows all Mr. Green's expenses for last month. If he spent $660 on his car, how much did he spend for his rent?

☐A. $700 ☐B. $740

☐C. $780 ☐D. $810

Mr. Green's monthly expenses

Bills 13%
Rent 27%
Others 28%
Car 22%
Foods 10%

39) If 150% of a number is 75, then what is the 90% of that number?

☐A. 45 ☐B. 50

☐C. 70 ☐D.85

40) A football team had $20,000 to spend on supplies. The team spent $14,000 on new balls. New sport shoes cost $120 each. Which of the following inequalities represent the number of new shoes the team can purchase.

☐A. $120x + 14,000 \leq 20,000$ ☐B. $120x + 14,000 \geq 20,000$

☐C. $14,000x + 120 \leq 20,000$ ☐D. $14,000x + 12,0 \geq 20,000$

**End of STAAR Mathematics Practice Test 1.**

# STAAR Mathematics Practice Test 2

# 2020

## Grade 8

**Total number of questions:** 40

**Total time to complete the test:** No time limit

**You may use a calculator on this practice test.**

# *STAAR Grade 8 Mathematics Formula Sheet*

## LINEAR EQUATIONS

| | |
|---|---|
| **Slope – intercept form** | $y = mx + b$ |
| **Direct Variation** | $y = kx$ |
| **Slope of a Line** | $m = \dfrac{y_2 - y_1}{x_2 - x_1}$ |

## CIRCUMFERENCE

| | |
|---|---|
| **Circle** | $C = 2\pi r$ or $C = \pi d$ |

## AREA

| | |
|---|---|
| Triangle | $A = \dfrac{1}{2}bh$ |
| Parallelogram | $A = bh$ |
| Trapezoid | $A = \dfrac{1}{2}h(b_1 + b_2)$ |
| Circle | $A = \pi r^2$ |

## SURFACE AREA

| | Lateral | Total |
|---|---|---|
| Prism | $S = Ph$ | $S = Ph + 2B$ |
| Cylinder | $S = 2\pi rh$ | $S = 2\pi rh + 2\pi r^2$ |

## VOLUME

| | |
|---|---|
| Prism or Cylinder | $V = Bh$ |
| Pyramid or Cone | $V = \dfrac{1}{3}Bh$ |
| Sphere | $V = \dfrac{4}{3}\pi r^3$ |

## ADDITIONAL INFORMATION

| | |
|---|---|
| Pythagorean theorem | $a^2 + b^2 = c^2$ |
| Simple interest | $I = prt$ |
| Compound Interest | $A = p(1 + r)^t$ |

1) If $x$ is directly proportional to the square of $y$, and $y = 2$ when $x = 12$, then when $x = 75$ $y = ?$

   ☐A. $\frac{1}{5}$                        ☐B. 1

   ☐C. 5                                    ☐D. 12

2) Jack earns $616 for his first 44 hours of work in a week and is then paid 1.5 times his regular hourly rate for any additional hours. This week, Jack needs $826 to pay his rent, bills and other expenses. How many hours must he work to make enough money in this week?

   ☐A. 40                                   ☐B. 53

   ☐C. 48                                   ☐D. 54

**Questions 3, 4 and 5 are based on the following data**

### Types of air pollutions in 10 cities of a country

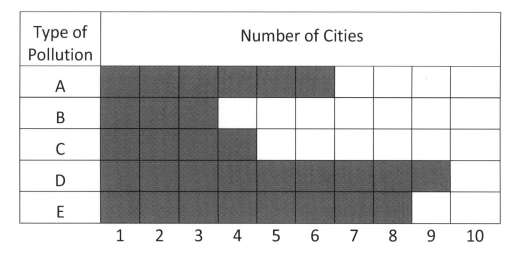

3) If $a$ is the mean (average) of the number of cities in each pollution type category, $b$ is the mode, and $c$ is the median of the number of cities in each pollution type category, then which of the following must be true?

   ☐A. $a < b < c$                          ☐B. $a = c$

   ☐C. $b < a < c$                          ☐C. $b < c = a$

4) What percent of cities are in the type of pollution $A, C$, and $E$ respectively?

☐A. 60%, 40%, 90%  ☐B. 30%, 40%, 90%

☐C. 30%, 40%, 60%  ☐D. 40%, 60%, 90%

5) How many cities should be added to type of pollutions $B$ until the ratio of cities in type of pollution $B$ to cities in type of pollution E will be 0.625?

☐A. 2  ☐B. 3

☐D. 4  ☐D. 5

6) In the following right triangle, if the sides $AB$ and $AC$ become twice longer, what will be the ratio of the perimeter of the triangle to its area?

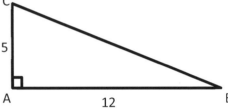

☐A. $\frac{1}{2}$  ☐B. 2

☐C. $\frac{1}{3}$  ☐D. 3

7) Which of the following is the same as: 0.000 000 000 000 042 121?

☐A. $4.2121 \times 10^{14}$  ☐B. $4.2121 \times 10^{-14}$

☐C. $42,121 \times 10^{-1}$  ☐D. $42.121 \times 10^{-13}$

8) A shirt costing $200 is discounted 15%. After a month, the shirt is discounted another 15%. Which of the following expressions can be used to find the selling price of the shirt?

☐A. $(200)(0.70)$  ☐B. $(200) - 200(0.30)$

☐C. $(200)(0.15) - (200)(0.15)$  ☐D. $(200)(0.85)(0.85)$

9) Which of the following points lies on the line $2x + 4y = 10$

☐A. $(2, 1)$  ☐B. $(-1, 3)$

☐C. $(-2, 2)$  ☐D. $(2, 2)$

10) What is the value of the expression? $5 + 8 \times (-2) - [4 + 22 \times 5] \div 6$

Write your answer in the box below.

11) What is the area of the shaded region if the diameter of the bigger circle is 12 inches and the diameter of the smaller circle is 8 inches?

☐A. $16\pi$  ☐B. $20\pi$

☐C. $36\pi$  ☐D. $80\pi$

12) A student gets an 85% on a test with 40 questions. How many answers did the student solve correctly?

☐ A. 25  ☐B. 28

☐ C. 34  ☐D. 36

13) If 60% of $A$ is 30% of $B$, then $B$ is what percent of $A$?

☐A. 3%  ☐B. 30%

☐ C. 200%  ☐D. 300%

14) How many possible outfit combinations come from six shirts, three slacks, and five ties?

Write your answer in the box below.

15) A ladder leans against a wall forming a 60° angle between the ground and the ladder. If the bottom of the ladder is 30 feet away from the wall, how long is the ladder?

☐A. 30 *feet*  ☐B. 40 *feet*

☐C. 50 *feet*  ☐D. 60 *feet*

16) When a number is subtracted from 24 and the difference is divided by that number, the result is 3. What is the value of the number?

☐A. 2                  ☐B. 4

☐C. 6                  ☐D. 12

17) An angle is equal to one fifth of its supplement. What is the measure of that angle in degrees?

☐A. 20°               ☐B. 30°

☐ C. 45°             ☐D. 60°

18) John traveled 150 $km$ in 6 hours and Alice traveled 180 $km$ in 4 hours. What is the ratio of the average speed of John to average speed of Alice?

☐A. 3 : 2             ☐B. 2 : 3

☐C. 5 : 9             ☐D. 5 : 6

19) What is the value of $y$ in the following system of equation?

$$3x - 4y = -40$$

$$-x + 2y = 10$$

Write your answer in the box below.

☐

20) In five successive hours, a car travels 40 $km$, 45 $km$, 50 $km$, 35 $km$ and 55 $km$. In the next five hours, it travels with an average speed of 50 $km\ per\ hour$. Find the total distance the car traveled in 10 hours.

☐A. 425 $km$           ☐B. 450 $km$

☐C. 475 $km$           ☐D. 500 $km$

21) How long does a 420–miles trip take moving at 50 miles per hour (*mph*)?

   ☐A. 4 *hours*                                   ☐B. 6 *hours and* 24 *minutes*

   ☐C. 8 *hours and* 24 *minutes*           ☐D. 8 *hours and* 30 *minutes*

22) Right triangle $ABC$ has two legs of lengths 6 *cm* ($AB$) and 8 *cm* ($AC$). What is the length of the third side ($BC$)?

   ☐ A. 4 *cm*                                       ☐ B. 6 *cm*

   ☐ C. 8 *cm*                                       ☐ D. 10 *cm*

23) The ratio of boys to girls in a school is 2: 3. If there are 600 students in a school, how many boys are in the school.

   Write your answer in the box below.

   ☐

24) The perimeter of the trapezoid below is 54. What is its area?

   Write your answer in the box below.

   ☐

25) Two third of 18 is equal to $\frac{2}{5}$ of what number?

   ☐A. 12                                             ☐B. 20

   ☐C. 30                                             ☐D. 60

26) The marked price of a computer is $D$ dollar. Its price decreased by 20% in January and later increased by 10% in February. What is the final price of the computer in D dollar?

   ☐A. 0.80$D$                                     ☐B. 0.88$D$

   ☐C. 0.90$D$                                     ☐D. 1.20$D$

27) In 1999, the average worker's income increased $2,000 per year starting from $24,000 annual salary. Which equation represents income greater than average? ($I$ = income, $x$ = number of years after 1999)

☐A. $I > 2,000\,x + 24,000$          ☐B. $I > -2,000\,x + 24,000$

☐C. $I < -2000\,x + 24,000$          ☐D. $I < 2,000\,x - 24,000$

28) From last year, the price of gasoline has increased from $1.25 per gallon to $1.75 per gallon. The new price is what percent of the original price?

☐A. 72%          ☐B. 120%

☐C. 140%          ☐D. 160%

29) A boat sails 40 miles south and then 30 miles east. How far is the boat from its start point?

☐A. $45\ miles$          ☐B. $50\ miles$

☐C. $60\ miles$          ☐D. $70\ miles$

30) Jason purchased a laptop for $529.72. The laptop is regularly priced at $646.00. What was the percent discount Jason received on the laptop?

☐A. 12%          ☐B. 18%

☐C. 20%          ☐D. 25%

31) A bag contains 18 balls: two green, five black, eight blue, a brown, a red and one white. If 17 balls are removed from the bag at random, what is the probability that a brown ball has been removed?

☐A. $\frac{1}{9}$          ☐B. $\frac{1}{6}$

☐C. $\frac{16}{17}$          ☐D. $\frac{17}{18}$

32) The average of five consecutive numbers is 38. What is the smallest number?

☐A. 38　　　　　　　　　　　　　　☐B. 36

☐C. 34　　　　　　　　　　　　　　☐D. 12

33) A rope weighs 600 grams per meter of length. What is the weight in kilograms of 12.2 meters of this rope? ($1\ kilograms\ =\ 1,000\ grams$)

☐A. 0.0732　　　　　　　　　　　　☐B. 0.732

☐C. 7.32　　　　　　　　　　　　　☐D. 7.320

34) A chemical solution contains 4% alcohol. If there is $32\ ml$ of alcohol, what is the volume of the solution?

☐A. $240\ ml$　　　　　　　　　　　☐B. $480\ ml$

☐C. $800\ ml$　　　　　　　　　　　☐D. $1200\ ml$

35) The average weight of 23 girls in a class is $60\ kg$ and the average weight of 32 boys in the same class is $62\ kg$. What is the average weight of all the 55 students in that class?

☐A. 60　　　　　　　　　　　　　　☐B. 61.16

☐C. 61.68　　　　　　　　　　　　☐D. 62.90

36) The price of a laptop is decreased by 20% to $360. What is its original price?

☐A. 320　　　　　　　　　　　　　☐B. 380

☐C. 400　　　　　　　　　　　　　☐D. 450

37) The radius of the following cylinder is 6 inches and its height is 12 inches. What is the surface area of the cylinder in square inches?

Write your answer in the box below. ($\pi$ equals 3.14)

```
┌─────────────────────────┐
│                         │
│                         │
└─────────────────────────┘
```

38) The average of $13, 15, 20$ and $x$ is $15$. What is the value of $x$?

Write your answer in the box below.

```
┌──────────────────────────────┐
│                              │
│                              │
└──────────────────────────────┘
```

39) In the $xy$-plane, the point $(1, 2)$ and $(-1, 6)$ are on line $A$. Which of the following points could also be on line $A$?

☐A. $(-1, 2)$            ☐B. $(3, 4)$

☐C. $(5, 7)$            ☐D. $(3, -2)$

40) A bank is offering $4.5\%$ simple interest on a savings account. If you deposit $\$9,000$, how much interest will you earn in five years?

☐A. $\$405$            ☐B. $\$720$

☐C. $\$2,025$            ☐D. $\$3,600$

**End of STAAR Mathematics Practice Test 2.**

# STAAR Mathematics Practice Test 3

# 2020

## Grade 8

**Total number of questions:** 40

**Total time to complete the test:** No time limit

## You may use a calculator on this practice test.

# *STAAR Grade 8 Mathematics Formula Sheet*

| LINEAR EQUATIONS | |
|---|---|
| **Slope – intercept form** | $y = mx + b$ |
| **Direct Variation** | $y = kx$ |
| **Slope of a Line** | $m = \dfrac{y_2 - y_1}{x_2 - x_1}$ |

| CIRCUMFERENCE | |
|---|---|
| **Circle** | $C = 2\pi r$ or $C = \pi d$ |

| AREA | |
|---|---|
| Triangle | $A = \dfrac{1}{2}bh$ |
| Parallelogram | $A = bh$ |
| Trapezoid | $A = \dfrac{1}{2}h(b_1 + b_2)$ |
| Circle | $A = \pi r^2$ |

| SURFACE AREA | | |
|---|---|---|
| | Lateral | Total |
| Prism | $S = Ph$ | $S = Ph + 2B$ |
| Cylinder | $S = 2\pi rh$ | $S = 2\pi rh + 2\pi r^2$ |

| VOLUME | |
|---|---|
| Prism or Cylinder | $V = Bh$ |
| Pyramid or Cone | $V = \dfrac{1}{3}Bh$ |
| Sphere | $V = \dfrac{4}{3}\pi r^3$ |

| ADDITIONAL INFORMATION | |
|---|---|
| Pythagorean theorem | $a^2 + b^2 = c^2$ |
| Simple interest | $I = prt$ |
| Compound Interest | $A = p(1 + r)^t$ |

1) The capacity of a red box is 20% bigger than the capacity of a blue box. If the red box can hold 30 equal sized books, how many of the same books can the blue box hold?

☐A. 9                                ☐B. 15

☐C. 21                             ☐D. 25

2) The sum of six different negative integers is $-70$. If the smallest of these integers is $-15$, what is the largest possible value of one of the other five integers?

☐A. $-14$                           ☐B. $-10$

☐C. $-5$                            ☐D. $-1$

3) $[6 \times (-24) + 8] - (-4) + [4 \times 5] \div 2 = ?$

Write your answer in the box below.

4) Which of the following is equal to the expression below?

$$(2x + 2y)(2x - y)$$

☐A. $4x^2 - 2y^2$                     ☐B. $2x^2 + 6xy - 2y^2$

☐C. $4x^2 - 2xy - 2y^2$            ☐D. $4x^2 + 2xy - 2y^2$

5) What is the product of all possible values of $x$ in the following equation?

$$|x - 10| = 3$$

☐A. 3                                  ☐B. 7

☐C. 13                             ☐D. 91

6) What is the slope of a line that is perpendicular to the line $4x - 2y = 12$?

☐A. $-2$                            ☐B. $-\dfrac{1}{2}$

☐C. 4                                ☐D. 12

7) What is the value of the expression $5(x + 2y) + (2 - x)^2$ when $x = 3$ and $y = -2$ ?

    ☐A. $-4$                               ☐B. 20

    ☐C. 36                                ☐D. 50

8) Bob is 12 miles ahead of Mike running at 6.5 miles per hour and Mike is running at the speed of 8 miles per hour. How long does it take Bob to catch Mike?

    ☐A. 3 *hours*                      ☐B. 4 *hours*

    ☐C. 6 *hours*                      ☐D. 8 *hours*

9) 44 students took an exam and 11 of them failed. What percent of the students passed the exam?

    ☐A. 20%                             ☐B. 40%

    ☐C. 60%                             ☐D. 75%

10) Which of the following graphs represents the compound inequality $-1 \le 2x - 3 < 1$?

 ☐A.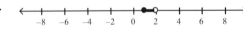

    ☐B.

    ☐C.

    ☐D.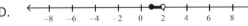

11) The diagonal of a rectangle is 13 inches long and the height of the rectangle is 5 inches. What is the area of the rectangle in inches?

    Write your answer in the box below.

12) The perimeter of the trapezoid below is $40\ cm$. What is its area?

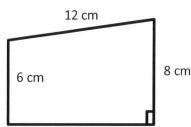

☐A. $576\ cm^2$                     ☐B. $98\ cm^2$

☐C. $40\ cm^2$                      ☐D. $24cm^2$

13) A card is drawn at random from a standard 52–card deck, what is the probability that the card is of Clubs? (The deck includes 13 of each suit clubs, diamonds, hearts, and spades)

☐A. $\dfrac{1}{3}$                     ☐B. $\dfrac{1}{4}$

☐C. $\dfrac{1}{6}$                     ☐D. $\dfrac{1}{52}$

14) The mean of 50 test scores was calculated as 80. But, it turned out that one of the scores was misread as 94 but it was 69. What is the mean?

☐A. 78.5                     ☐B. 79.5

☐C. 80.5                     ☐D. 88.5

15) Two dice are thrown simultaneously, what is the probability of getting a sum of 6 or 9?

☐A. $\dfrac{1}{3}$                     ☐B. $\dfrac{1}{4}$

☐C. $\dfrac{1}{6}$                     ☐D. $\dfrac{1}{12}$

16) A swimming pool holds 2,500 cubic feet of water. The swimming pool is 25 feet long and 10 feet wide. How deep is the swimming pool?
Write your answer in the box below. (<u>Don't write the measurement</u>)

17) Alice is choosing a menu for her lunch. She has 3 choices of appetizers, 5 choices of entrees, 6 choices of cake. How many different menu combinations are possible for her to choose?

☐A. 12                     ☐B. 32

☐C. 90                     ☐D. 120

18) Four one – foot rulers can be split among how many users to leave each with $\frac{1}{3}$ of a ruler?

☐A. 4                          ☐B. 6

☐C. 12                         ☐D. 24

19) What is the area of a square whose diagonal is 4?

☐A. 8                          ☐B. 32

☐C. 36                         ☐D. 64

20) Anita's trick–or–treat bag contains 15 pieces of chocolate, 10 suckers, 10 pieces of gum, 25 pieces of licorice. If she randomly pulls a piece of candy from her bag, what is the probability of her pulling out a piece of sucker?

☐A. $\frac{1}{3}$              ☐B. $\frac{1}{4}$

☐C. $\frac{1}{6}$             ☐D. $\frac{1}{12}$

21) The volume of a cube is less than $64\ m^3$. Which of the following can be the cube's side?

☐A. $2\ m$                    ☐B. $5\ m$

☐C. $4\ m$                    ☐D. $6\ m$

22) The perimeter of a rectangular yard is 72 meters. What is its length if its width is twice its length?

☐A. 12 meters                 ☐B. 18 meters

☐C. 20 meters                 ☐D. 24 meters

23) The average of 6 numbers is 10. The average of 4 of those numbers is 7. What is the average of the other two numbers.

☐A. 10                         ☐B. 12

☐C. 14                         ☐D. 16

24) What is the value of $x$ in the following system of equations?

$$2x + 5y = 11$$
$$4x - 2y = -26$$

☐A. $-1$                      ☐B. 1

☐C. $-4.5$                 ☐D. 4.5

25) The area of a circle is less than $81\pi \ ft^2$. Which of the following can be the diameter of the circle?

☐A. $28 ft$                 ☐B. $18 ft$

☐C. $20 ft$                 ☐D. $17 ft$

26) The ratio of boys and girls in a class is $4: 7$. If there are 55 students in the class, how many more boys should be enrolled to make the ratio $1: 1$?

☐A. 8                       ☐B. 10

☐C. 12                     ☐D. 15

27) A football team had \$20,000 to spend on supplies. The team spent \$10,000 on new balls. New sport shoes cost \$120 each. Which of the following inequalities represent the number of new shoes the team can purchase.

☐A. $120x + 10,000 \leq 20,000$        ☐B. $120x + 10,000 \geq 20,000$

☐C. $10,000x + 120 \leq 20,000$        ☐D. $10,000x + 12,0 \geq 20,000$

28) Jason needs an 70% average in his writing class to pass. On his first 4 exams, he earned scores of $68\%, 72\%, 85\%$, and $90\%$. What is the minimum score Jason can earn on his fifth and final test to pass?

Write your answer in the box below.

☐

29) What is the value of $x$ in the following equation? $\frac{2}{3}x + \frac{1}{6} = \frac{1}{2}$

☐A. 6

☐B. $\frac{1}{2}$

☐C. $\frac{1}{3}$

☐D. $\frac{1}{4}$

30) A bank is offering 3.5% simple interest on a savings account. If you deposit $14,000, how much interest will you earn in two years?

☐A. $490

☐B. $980

☐C. $4,200

☐D. $4,900

31) Simplify $5x^2y^3(2x^2y)^3 =$

☐A. $12x^4y^6$

☐B. $12x^8y^6$

☐C. $40x^4y^6$

☐D. $40x^8y^6$

32) What is the surface area of the cylinder below?

☐A. $28\,\pi\,in^2$

☐B. $37\,\pi\,in^2$

☐C. $40\,\pi\,in^2$

☐D. $288\,\pi\,in^2$

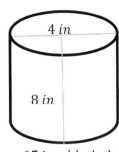

4 in

8 in

33) The average of four numbers is 48. If a fifth number that is greater than 65 is added, then, which of the following could be the new average?

☐A. 48

☐B. 51

☐C. 50

☐D. 52

34) A cruise line ship left Port $A$ and traveled 50 miles due west and then 120 miles due north. At this point, what is the shortest distance from the cruise to port $A$ in miles?

Write your answer in the box below.

35) What is the equivalent temperature of $140°F$ in Celsius? $C = \frac{5}{9}(F - 32)$

☐A. 32                              ☐B. 40

☐C. 48                              ☐D. 60

36) If 150% of a number is 75, then what is the 80% of that number?

☐A. 40                              ☐B. 50

☐C. 70                              ☐D.85

37) Simplify the expression. $(5x^3 - 8x^2 + 2x^4) - (4x^2 - 2x^4 + 2x^3)$

☐A. $4x^4 + 3x^3 - 12x^2$            ☐B. $4x^3 - 12x^2$

☐C. $4x^4 - 3x^3 - 12x^2$            ☐D. $8x^3 - 12x^2$

38) In two successive years, the population of a town is increased by 10% and 20%. What percent of the population is increased after two years?

☐A. 30%                             ☐B. 32%

☐C. 34%                             ☐D. 68%

39) Last week 25,000 fans attended a football match. This week three times as many bought tickets, but one sixth of them cancelled their tickets. How many are attending this week?

☐A. 48,000                          ☐B. 54,000

☐C. 62,500                          ☐D. 72,000

40) Which graph shows a non-proportional linear relationship between $x$ and $y$?

☐ A.

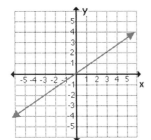

☐ B.

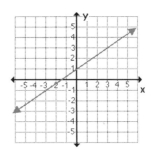

☐ C.

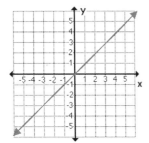

☐ D.

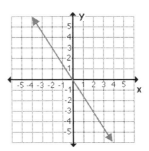

**End of STAAR Mathematics Practice Test 3.**

# STAAR Mathematics Practice Test 4

# 2020

## Grade 8

**Total number of questions:** 40

**Total time to complete the test:** No time limit

## You may use a calculator on this practice test.

# *STAAR Grade 8 Mathematics Formula Sheet*

| LINEAR EQUATIONS | |
|---|---|
| **Slope – intercept form** | $y = mx + b$ |
| **Direct Variation** | $y = kx$ |
| **Slope of a Line** | $m = \dfrac{y_2 - y_1}{x_2 - x_1}$ |

| CIRCUMFERENCE | |
|---|---|
| **Circle** | $C = 2\pi r$ or $C = \pi d$ |

| AREA | |
|---|---|
| Triangle | $A = \dfrac{1}{2}bh$ |
| Parallelogram | $A = bh$ |
| Trapezoid | $A = \dfrac{1}{2}h(b_1 + b_2)$ |
| Circle | $A = \pi r^2$ |

| SURFACE AREA | Lateral | Total |
|---|---|---|
| Prism | $S = Ph$ | $S = Ph + 2B$ |
| Cylinder | $S = 2\pi rh$ | $S = 2\pi rh + 2\pi r^2$ |

| VOLUME | |
|---|---|
| Prism or Cylinder | $V = Bh$ |
| Pyramid or Cone | $V = \dfrac{1}{3}Bh$ |
| Sphere | $V = \dfrac{4}{3}\pi r^3$ |

| ADDITIONAL INFORMATION | |
|---|---|
| Pythagorean theorem | $a^2 + b^2 = c^2$ |
| Simple interest | $I = prt$ |
| Compound Interest | $A = p(1 + r)^t$ |

1) The Jackson Library is ordering some bookshelves. If $x$ is the number of bookshelves the library wants to order, which each costs \$100 and there is a one-time delivery charge of \$800, which of the following represents the total cost, in dollar, per bookshelf?

☐A. $100x + 800$                 ☐B. $100 + 800x$

☐C. $\frac{100x+800}{100}$                ☐D. $\frac{100x+800}{x}$

2) What is the sum of $\sqrt{x-7}$ and $\sqrt{x}-7$ when $\sqrt{x}=4$?

☐A. $-3$                      ☐B. $-1$

☐C. $0$                        ☐D. $3$

3) In the following figure, point Q lies on line n, what is the value of $y$ if $x = 35$?

☐A. 15                      ☐B. 25

☐C. 35                      ☐D. 45

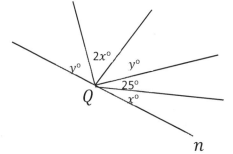

4) What is the value of $|-12-5| - |-8+2|$?

☐A. 11                      ☐B. $-11$

☐C. 23                      ☐D. $-23$

5) In the figure below, what is the value of $x$?

☐A. 43                      ☐B. 67

☐C. 77                      ☐D. 90

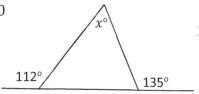

6) The following table represents the value of $x$ and function $f(x)$. Which of the following could be the equation of the function $f(x)$?

☐A. $f(x) = x^2 - 5$            ☐B. $f(x) = x^2 - 1$

☐C. $f(x) = \sqrt{x+2}$          ☐D. $f(x) = \sqrt{x} + 4$

| $x$ | $f(x)$ |
|---|---|
| 1 | 5 |
| 4 | 6 |
| 9 | 7 |
| 16 | 8 |

7) If $3x - 5 = 8.5$, What is the value of $5x + 3$?

☐A. 13                      ☐B. 15.5

☐C. 20.5                   ☐D. 25.5

8) What is the area of an isosceles right triangle that has one leg that measures $6\ cm$?

☐A. $6\ cm^2$                                          ☐B. $12\ cm^2$

☐C. $18\ cm^2$                                      ☐D. $36\ cm^2$

9) A shirt costing \$500 is discounted 25%. After a month, the shirt is discounted another 15%. Which of the following expressions can be used to find the selling price of the shirt?

☐A. $(500)\,(0.60)$                           ☐B. $(500) - 500\,(0.40)$

☐C. $(500)(0.25) - (200)\,(0.15)$     ☐D. $(500)\,(0.75)\,(0.85)$

10) Which of the following points lies on the line with equation $3x + 5y = 7$ ?

☐A. $(2, 1)$                                      ☐B. $(-1, 2)$

☐C. $(-2, 2)$                                  ☐D. $(2, 2)$

11) The average of $13, 15, 20$ and $x$ is $18$. What is the value of $x$?

Write your answer in the box below.

```
┌─────────────────────────┐
│                         │
│                         │
└─────────────────────────┘
```

12) When a number is subtracted from 32 and the difference is divided by that number, the result is 3. What is the value of the number?

☐A. 2                                            ☐B. 4

☐C. 8                                            ☐D. 12

13) An angle is equal to one ninth of its supplement. What is the measure of that angle?

☐A.18                                           ☐B. 24

☐ C. 36                                         ☐D. 45

14) John traveled 140 $km$ in 7 hours and Alice traveled 180 $km$ in 4 hours. What is the ratio of the average speed of John to average speed of Alice?

☐A. 3 : 2                                    ☐B. 2 : 3

☐C. 4 : 9                                    ☐D. 5 : 6

15) Right triangle $ABC$ has two legs of lengths 9 $cm$ ($AB$) and 12 $cm$ ($AC$). What is the length of the third side (BC)?

☐ A. 6 $cm$                                 ☐ B. 8 $cm$

☐ C. 14 $cm$                                ☐ D. 15 $cm$

16) The area of a circle is less than 64 $\pi$. Which of the following can be the circumference of the circle?

☐A. 8 $\pi$                                 ☐B. 32 $\pi$

☐C. 16 $\pi$                                ☐D. 64 $\pi$

17) What is the value of $y$ in the following system of equation?

$$3x - 4y = -16$$

$$-x + 2y = 10$$

Write your answer in the box below.

┌─────────────────────┐
│                     │
└─────────────────────┘

18) The price of a car was $28,000 in 2012. In 2013, the price of that car was $18,200. What was the rate of depreciation of the price of car per year?

☐ A.20%                                    ☐B. 30%

☐ C.35%                                    ☐D. 40%

19) The width of a box is one third of its length. The height of the box is one third of its width. If the length of the box is $36\ cm$, what is the volume of the box?

☐A.$81\ cm^3$          ☐ B. $162\ cm^3$

☐C.$243\ cm^3$        ☐ D. $1,728\ cm^3$

20) How many possible outfit combinations come from six shirts, four slacks, and five ties?

Write your answer in the box below.

21) A bank is offering 4.5% simple interest on a savings account. If you deposit $8,000, how much interest will you earn in five years?

☐A. $360          ☐B. $720

☐C. $1,800        ☐D. $3,600

22) 35 is What percent of 20?

☐A. 20%          ☐B. 25%

☐C. 175%        ☐D. 180%

23) The perimeter of the trapezoid below is 64. What is its area?

Write your answer in the box below.

18

12               14

24) In five successive hours, a car travels $46\ km, 45\ km, 50\ km, 35\ km$ and $55\ km$. In the next five hours, it travels with an average speed of $50\ km\ per\ hour$. Find the total distance the car traveled in 10 hours.

☐A. $425\ km$          ☐B. $451\ km$

☐C. $481\ km$        ☐D.$501\ km$

25) In the $xy$-plane, the point $(4,3)$ and $(3,2)$ are on line $A$. Which of the following points could also be on line $A$?

☐A. $(-1, 2)$          ☐B. $(3, 4)$

☐C. $(5, 7)$          ☐D. $(-1, -2)$

26) The marked price of a computer is $D$ dollar. Its price decreased by 15% in January and later increased by 10% in February. What is the final price of the computer in $D$ dollar?

☐A. $0.80\ D$          ☐B. $0.88\ D$

☐C. $0.93\ D$          ☐D. $1.20\ D$

27) What is the distance between the points $(1, 3)$ and $(-2, 7)$?

☐A. 3          ☐B. 4

☐C. 5          ☐D. 6

28) The ratio of boys to girls in a school is $2:3$. If there are 500 students in a school, how many boys are in the school.

Write your answer in the box below.

```
┌─────────────────────────┐
│                         │
└─────────────────────────┘
```

29) Sophia purchased a sofa for $530.40. The sofa is regularly priced at $624. What was the percent discount Sophia received on the sofa?

☐A. 12%          ☐B. 15%

☐C. 20%          ☐D. 25%

30) A bag contains 20 balls: four green, five black, eight blue, a brown, a red and one white. If 19 balls are removed from the bag at random, what is the probability that a brown ball has been removed?

☐A. $\dfrac{1}{9}$          ☐B. $\dfrac{1}{20}$

☐C. $\dfrac{4}{5}$          ☐D. $\dfrac{19}{20}$

31) The average of five consecutive numbers is 36. What is the smallest number?

☐A. 38                             ☐B. 36

☐C. 34                             ☐D. 12

32) A rope weighs 600 grams per meter of length. What is the weight in kilograms of 14.2 meters of this rope? ($1\ kilograms = 1,000\ grams$)

☐A. 0.0852                     ☐B. 0.852

☐C. 8.52                        ☐D. 85.20

33) A chemical solution contains 8% alcohol. If there is 38.4 $ml$ of alcohol, what is the volume of the solution?

☐A. 240 $ml$                    ☐B. 480 $ml$

☐C. 600 $ml$                    ☐D. 1200 $ml$

34) The average weight of 18 girls in a class is 65 $kg$ and the average weight of 32 boys in the same class is 62 $kg$. What is the average weight of all the 50 students in that class?

☐A. 60                             ☐B. 62.28

☐C. 62.68                       ☐D. 63.08

35) What is the median of these numbers? $3, 8, 13, 7, 15, 18, 5$

☐A. 7                               ☐B. 8

☐C. 13                             ☐D. 15

36) The radius of the following cylinder is 5 inches and its height is 12 inches. What is the surface area of the cylinder in square inches?

Write your answer in the box below. ($\pi$ equals 3.14)

```
┌─────────────────────────┐
│                         │
└─────────────────────────┘
```

37) In 1999, the average worker's income increased $3,000 per year starting from $24,000 annual salary. Which equation represents income greater than average? ($I$ = income, $x$ = number of years after 1999)

☐A. $I > 3000\,x + 24000$

☐B. $I > -3000\,x + 24000$

☐C. $I < -3000\,x + 24000$

☐D. $I < 3000\,x - 24000$

38) From last year, the price of gasoline has increased from $1.40 per gallon to $1.75 per gallon. The new price is what percent of the original price?

☐A. 72%

☐B. 125%

☐C. 140%

☐D. 160%

39) A boat sails 12 miles south and then 16 miles east. How far is the boat from its start point?

☐A. 18 miles

☐B. 20 miles

☐C. 24 miles

☐D. 28 miles

40) Which graph corresponds to the following inequalities?

$$y \leq x + 4$$
$$2x + y \leq -4$$

□A.                                     □B.

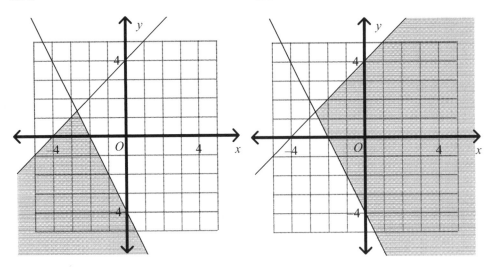

□C.                                     □D.

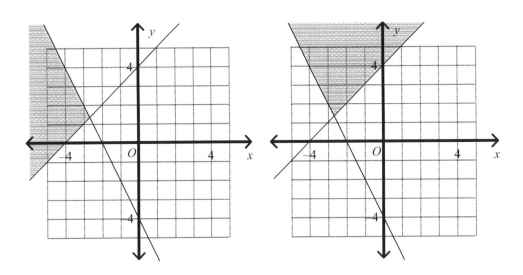

**End of STAAR Mathematics Practice Test 4.**

# STAAR Mathematics Practice Test 5

# 2020

## Grade 8

**Total number of questions:** 40

**Total time to complete the test:** No time limit

## You may use a calculator on this practice test.

# *STAAR Grade 8 Mathematics Formula Sheet*

## LINEAR EQUATIONS

| | |
|---|---|
| **Slope – intercept form** | $y = mx + b$ |
| **Direct Variation** | $y = kx$ |
| **Slope of a Line** | $m = \dfrac{y_2 - y_1}{x_2 - x_1}$ |

## CIRCUMFERENCE

| | |
|---|---|
| **Circle** | $C = 2\pi r$ or $C = \pi d$ |

## AREA

| | |
|---|---|
| Triangle | $A = \dfrac{1}{2}bh$ |
| Parallelogram | $A = bh$ |
| Trapezoid | $A = \dfrac{1}{2}h(b_1 + b_2)$ |
| Circle | $A = \pi r^2$ |

## SURFACE AREA

| | Lateral | Total |
|---|---|---|
| Prism | $S = Ph$ | $S = Ph + 2B$ |
| Cylinder | $S = 2\pi rh$ | $S = 2\pi rh + 2\pi r^2$ |

## VOLUME

| | |
|---|---|
| Prism or Cylinder | $V = Bh$ |
| Pyramid or Cone | $V = \dfrac{1}{3}Bh$ |
| Sphere | $V = \dfrac{4}{3}\pi r^3$ |

## ADDITIONAL INFORMATION

| | |
|---|---|
| Pythagorean theorem | $a^2 + b^2 = c^2$ |
| Simple interest | $I = prt$ |
| Compound Interest | $A = p(1 + r)^t$ |

1) Which of the following equations has a graph that is a straight line?
   ☐A. $y = 3x^2 + 9$                 ☐B. $x^2 + y^2 = 1$

   ☐C. $4x - 2y = 2x$                 ☐D. $7x + 2xy = 6$

2) Triangle $ABC$ is graphed on a coordinate grid with vertices at $A\,(-3, -2), B\,(-1, 4)$ and $C\,(7, 9)$. Triangle $ABC$ is reflected over $x$ axes to create triangle $A'\,B'\,C'$.
   Which order pair represents the coordinate of $C'$?
   ☐A. $(7, 9)$                       ☐B. $(-7, -9)$
   ☐C. $(-7, 9)$                      ☐D. $(7, -9)$

3) What is the volume of the following triangular prism?
   Write your answer in the box below.

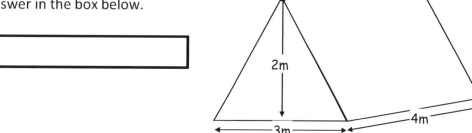

4) Which of the following is the solution of the following inequality?
   $$2x + 4 > 11x - 12.5 - 3.5x$$
   ☐A. $x < 3$                        ☐B. $x > 3$

   ☐C. $x \le 4$                      ☐D. $x \ge 4$

5) If $3x - 5 = 8.5$, what is the value of $6x + 3$ ?
   ☐A. 13                             ☐B. 15.5

   ☐C. 20.5                           ☐D. 30

6) What is the area of an isosceles right triangle that has one leg that measures $8\ cm$?

   ☐A. $6\ cm^2$                      ☐B. $12\ cm^2$

   ☐C. $18\ cm^2$                     ☐D. $32\ cm^2$

7) A shirt costing \$600 is discounted 25%. After a month, the shirt is discounted another 15%. Which of the following expressions can be used to find the selling price of the shirt?

   ☐A. $(600)(0.60)$                  ☐B. $(600) - 600\,(0.40)$

   ☐C. $(600)(0.25) - (200)(0.15)$    ☐D. $(600)(0.75)(0.85)$

8) Which of the following points lies on the line with equation $3x + 5y = 11$ ?

☐A. $(2, 1)$                         ☐B. $(-1, 2)$

☐C. $(-2, 2)$                     ☐D. $(2, 2)$

9) What is the value of expression? $-15 + 6 \times (-5) - [4 + 22 \times (-4)] \div 2 = ?$

Write your answer in the box below.

┌────────────────────────────────┐
│                                │
└────────────────────────────────┘

10) A chemical solution contains 6% alcohol. If there is $24\ ml$ of alcohol, what is the volume of the solution?

☐A. $240\ ml$                     ☐B. $400\ ml$

☐C. $600\ ml$                     ☐D. $1200\ ml$

11) The average weight of 18 girls in a class is $60\ kg$ and the average weight of 32 boys in the same class is $62\ kg$. What is the average weight of all the 50 students in that class?

☐A. 60                           ☐B. 61.28

☐C. 61.68                     ☐D. 62.90

12) The radius of the following cylinder is 8 inches and its height is 16 inches. What is the surface area of the cylinder in square inches?

Write your answer in the box below. (π equals 3.14)

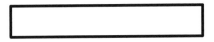

13) In 1999, the average worker's income increased $2,000 per year starting from $27,000 annual salary. Which equation represents income greater than average? ($I$ = income, $x$ = number of years after 1999)

☐A. $I > 2,000\ x + 27,000$           ☐B. $I > -2,000\ x + 27,000$

☐C. $I < -2,000\ x + 27,000$        ☐D. $I < 2,000\ x - 27,000$

14) What is the value of $y$ in the following system of equation?

$$3x - 4y = -20$$

$$-x + 2y = 10$$

Write your answer in the box below.

15) What is the area of a square whose diagonal is 6 meters?

☐ A. 20 $m^2$            ☐ B. 18 $m^2$

☐ C. 12 $m^2$            ☐ D. 10 $m^2$

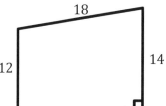

16) The width of a box is one third of its length. The height of the box is half of its width. If the length of the box is 24 $cm$, what is the volume of the box?

☐ A. 81 $cm^3$            ☐ B. 162 $cm^3$

☐ C. 243 $cm^3$           ☐ D. 768 $cm^3$

17) If 60% of $A$ is 20% of $B$, then $B$ is what percent of $A$?

☐ A. 3%                ☐ B. 30%

☐ C. 200%            ☐ D. 300%

18) A bank is offering 2.5% simple interest on a savings account. If you deposit $8,000, how much interest will you earn in five years?

☐ A. $360             ☐ B. $720

☐ C. $1,000          ☐ D. $3,600

19) The perimeter of the trapezoid below is 50. What is its area?

Write your answer in the box below.

20) In five successive hours, a car travels $40\ km$, $45\ km$, $50\ km$, $35\ km$ and $55\ km$. In the next five hours, it travels with an average speed of $45\ km\ per\ hour$. Find the total distance the car traveled in $10\ hours$.

  ☐A. $425\ km$          ☐B. $450\ km$

  ☐C. $475\ km$          ☐D.$500\ km$

21) Which of the following points lies on the line $4x + 6y = 20$?

  ☐A. $(2, 1)$          ☐B. $(-1, 3)$

  ☐C. $(-2, 2)$         ☐D. $(2, 2)$

22) Two third of 15 is equal to $\dfrac{2}{5}$ of what number?

  ☐A. 12           ☐B. 20

  ☐C. 25           ☐D. 60

23) The marked price of a computer is $D$ dollar. Its price decreased by 20% in January and later increased by 15% in February. What is the final price of the computer in $D$ dollar?

  ☐A. $0.80\ D$         ☐B. $0.88\ D$

  ☐C. $0.92\ D$         ☐D. $1.20$

24) A $45 shirt now selling for $28 is discounted by about what percent?

  ☐A. 20%          ☐B. 37.7%

  ☐C. 40%          ☐D. 60%

25) Which of the following could be the product of two consecutive prime numbers?

  ☐A. 2           ☐B. 14

  ☐C. 10           ☐D. 15

26) The ratio of boys to girls in a school is $2:3$. If there are $400$ students in a school, how many boys are in the school.

Write your answer in the box below.

27) Sophia purchased a sofa for $530.40. The sofa is regularly priced at $631. What was the percent discount Sophia received on the sofa?

□A. 12%
□B. 16%

□C. 20%
□D. 25%

28) The score of Emma was half as that of Ava and the score of Mia was twice that of Ava. If the score of Mia was 60, what is the score of Emma?

□A. 12
□B. 15

□C. 20
□D. 30

29) A bag contains 21 balls: two green, six black, eight blue, two brown, two red and one white. If 20 balls are removed from the bag at random, what is the probability that a white ball has been removed?

□A. $\frac{1}{9}$
□B. $\frac{1}{6}$

□C. $\frac{4}{5}$
□D. $\frac{20}{21}$

30) The average of $13, 15, 20$ and $x$ is $25$. What is the value of $x$?

Write your answer in the box below.

31) An angle is equal to one fourth of its supplement. What is the measure of that angle?

□A. 18
□B. 24

□C. 36
□D. 45

32) Right triangle $ABC$ has two legs of lengths $5\ cm$ $(AB)$ and $12\ cm$ $(AC)$. What is the length of the third side $(BC)$?

☐ A. $6\ cm$                        ☐ B. $8\ cm$

☐ C. $13\ cm$                       ☐ D. $15\ cm$

33) The area of a circle is less than $49\pi$. Which of the following can be the circumference of the circle?

☐A. $8\pi$                          ☐B. $16\pi$

☐C. $14\pi$                         ☐D. $32\pi$

34) If $2y + 6 < 30$, then $y$ could be equal to?

☐A. 15                             ☐B. 12

☐C. 14                             ☐D. 8

35) From last year, the price of a table has increased from $125.00 to $185.00. The new price is what percent of the original price?

☐A. 72%                            ☐B. 120%

☐C. 148%                           ☐D. 160%

36) A boat sails 80 $miles$ south and then 150 $miles$ east. How far is the boat from its start point?

☐A. 160 $miles$                    ☐B. 170 $miles$

☐C. 200 $miles$                    ☐D. 230 $miles$

37) Which graph does not represent $y$ as a function of $x$?

☐ A.

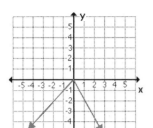

☐ B.

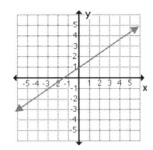

☐ C.

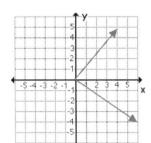

☐ D.

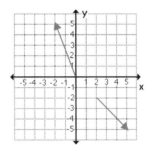

38) Which of the following is equivalent to $13 < -3x - 2 < 22$ ?

☐A. $-8 < x < -5$          ☐B. $5 < x < 8$

☐C. $\frac{11}{3} < x < \frac{20}{3}$          ☐D. $\frac{-2}{3} < x < \frac{-11}{3}$

39) In a certain bookshelf of a library, there are 35 biology books, 95 history books, and 80 language books. What is the ratio of the number of biology books to the total number of books in this bookshelf?

☐A. $\frac{1}{4}$          ☐B. $\frac{1}{6}$

☐C. $\frac{2}{7}$          ☐D. $\frac{3}{8}$

40) Which of the following point is the solution of the system of equations?

$$\begin{cases} 5x + y = 9 \\ 10x - 7y = -18 \end{cases}$$

☐A. (2, 4)      ☐B. (2, 2)

☐C. (1, 4)      ☐D. (0, 4)

## End of STAAR Mathematics Practice Test 5.

# STAAR Mathematics Practice Tests

## Answer Keys

Now, it's time to review your results to see where you went wrong and what areas you need to improve.

| STAAR Math Practice Test 1 | | | | STAAR Math Practice Test 2 | | | |
|---|---|---|---|---|---|---|---|
| 1 | C | 21 | B | 1 | C | 21 | C |
| 2 | B | 22 | A | 2 | D | 22 | D |
| 3 | D | 23 | D | 3 | C | 23 | 240 |
| 4 | B | 24 | C | 4 | A | 24 | 130 |
| 5 | −64 | 25 | B | 5 | A | 25 | C |
| 6 | A | 26 | B | 6 | A | 26 | B |
| 7 | B | 27 | D | 7 | B | 27 | A |
| 8 | C | 28 | 28 | 8 | D | 28 | C |
| 9 | 2.5 | 29 | C | 9 | B | 29 | B |
| 10 | D | 30 | A | 10 | −30 | 30 | B |
| 11 | A | 31 | 60 | 11 | B | 31 | D |
| 12 | C | 32 | D | 12 | C | 32 | B |
| 13 | C | 33 | B | 13 | C | 33 | C |
| 14 | 97.6 | 34 | D | 14 | 90 | 34 | C |
| 15 | C | 35 | C | 15 | D | 35 | B |
| 16 | D | 36 | 170 | 16 | C | 36 | D |
| 17 | 8 | 37 | B | 17 | B | 37 | 678.24 |
| 18 | C | 38 | D | 18 | C | 38 | 12 |
| 19 | A | 39 | A | 19 | −5 | 39 | D |
| 20 | B | 40 | A | 20 | C | 40 | C |

**STAAR Math Practice Test 3**

| | | | |
|---|---|---|---|
| 1 | D | 21 | A |
| 2 | C | 22 | A |
| 3 | −122 | 23 | D |
| 4 | D | 24 | C |
| 5 | D | 25 | D |
| 6 | B | 26 | D |
| 7 | A | 27 | A |
| 8 | D | 28 | 35 |
| 9 | D | 29 | B |
| 10 | D | 30 | B |
| 11 | 60 | 31 | D |
| 12 | B | 32 | C |
| 13 | B | 33 | D |
| 14 | B | 34 | 130 |
| 15 | B | 35 | D |
| 16 | 10 | 36 | A |
| 17 | C | 37 | A |
| 18 | C | 38 | B |
| 19 | A | 39 | C |
| 20 | C | 40 | B |

**STAAR Math Practice Test 4**

| | | | |
|---|---|---|---|
| 1 | C | 21 | C |
| 2 | C | 22 | C |
| 3 | B | 23 | 260 |
| 4 | A | 24 | C |
| 5 | B | 25 | D |
| 6 | D | 26 | C |
| 7 | D | 27 | C |
| 8 | C | 28 | 200 |
| 9 | D | 29 | B |
| 10 | B | 30 | D |
| 11 | 24 | 31 | C |
| 12 | C | 32 | C |
| 13 | A | 33 | B |
| 14 | C | 34 | D |
| 15 | D | 35 | B |
| 16 | A | 36 | 533.8 |
| 17 | 7 | 37 | A |
| 18 | C | 38 | B |
| 19 | D | 39 | B |
| 20 | 120 | 40 | A |

**STAAR Math Practice Test 5**

| | | | |
|---|---|---|---|
| **1** | C | **21** | D |
| **2** | D | **22** | C |
| **3** | 12 | **23** | C |
| **4** | A | **24** | B |
| **5** | D | **25** | D |
| **6** | D | **26** | 160 |
| **7** | D | **27** | B |
| **8** | A | **28** | B |
| **9** | −3 | **29** | D |
| **10** | B | **30** | 52 |
| **11** | B | **31** | C |
| **12** | 1,205.76 | **32** | C |
| **13** | A | **33** | A |
| **14** | 5 | **34** | D |
| **15** | B | **35** | C |
| **16** | D | **36** | B |
| **17** | D | **37** | C |
| **18** | C | **38** | A |
| **19** | 78 | **39** | B |
| **20** | B | **40** | C |

# How to score your test

The basic score on each STAAR test is the raw score, which is simply the number of questions correct. On the STAAR test each subject test should be passed individually. It means that you must meet the standard on each section of the test. If you failed one subject test but did well enough on another, that's still not a passing score.

There are four possible scores that you can receive on the STAAR Math Grade 8 Test:

**Do Not Meet:** This indicates that your score is lower than the passing score. If you do not pass, you can reschedule to retake any the STAAR Math test. Students have three opportunities to retake test(s) and receive remedial help if they don't pass.

**Approaches:** This score indicates that your score meets the standard of t

**Met the Standard:** This indicates that your score meets Texas state standards for that subject.

**Commended Performance:** This indicates that you've mastered the skills that would be taught in your grade.

There are approximately 40 questions on STAAR Mathematics for grade 8. Similar to other subject areas, you will need a minimum score to pass the Mathematics Test. There are approximately 40 raw score points on the STAAR math test. The raw points correspond with correct answers. This will then be converted into your scaled score. Approximately, you need to get 28 out of 40 raw score to pass the STAAR Mathematics for grade 8.

To score your STAAR Mathematics practice tests, first find your raw score. There were 40 questions on each STAAR Mathematics practice test in this book. All questions have one point. Use the following table to convert your raw score to the scale score.

| Raw Score | Scale Score | Result | Percentile |
|---|---|---|---|
| 0 | 1065 | | 0 |
| 1 | 1197 | | 0 |
| 2 | 1276 | | 0 |
| 3 | 1324 | | 0 |
| 4 | 1359 | | 0 |
| 5 | 1387 | | 0 |
| 6 | 1411 | | 0 |
| 7 | 1432 | | 1 |
| 8 | 1451 | | 2 |
| 9 | 1468 | | 3 |
| 10 | 1484 | **Do Not Meet** | 4 |
| 11 | 1499 | | 6 |
| 12 | 1513 | | 8 |
| 13 | 1526 | | 10 |
| 14 | 1539 | | 12 |
| 15 | 1552 | | 14 |
| 16 | 1564 | | 16 |
| 17 | 1576 | | 19 |
| 18 | 1588 | | 22 |
| 19 | 1595 | | 25 |
| 20 | 1611 | | 27 |
| 21 | 1622 | | 30 |
| 22 | 1634 | | 34 |
| 23 | 1645 | **Approaches** | 37 |
| 24 | 1657 | | 41 |
| 25 | 1669 | | 44 |
| 26 | 1681 | | 48 |
| 27 | 1693 | | 52 |
| 28 | 1700 | | 55 |
| 29 | 1719 | | 60 |
| 30 | 1733 | | 64 |
| 31 | 1747 | | 68 |
| 32 | 1762 | **Meets** | 72 |
| 33 | 1779 | | 76 |
| 34 | 1796 | | 79 |
| 35 | 1815 | | 83 |
| 36 | 1836 | | 87 |
| 37 | 1854 | | 89 |
| 38 | 1889 | | 93 |
| 39 | 1925 | **Masters** | 96 |
| 40 or more | 1973-2185 | | 98-100 |

# STAAR Mathematics Practice Tests
# Answers and Explanations

## STAAR Mathematics Practice Test 1

### Answers and Explanations

**1) Choice C is correct**

The perimeter of the rectangle is: $2x + 2y = 30 \rightarrow x + y = 15 \rightarrow x = 15 - y$

The area of the rectangle is: $x \times y = 50 \rightarrow (15 - y)(y) = 50 \rightarrow y^2 - 15y + 50 = 0$

Solve the quadratic equation by factoring method. $(y - 5)(y - 10) = 0 \rightarrow y = 5$ (Unacceptable, because $y$ must be greater than 5) or $y = 10$

If $y = 10 \rightarrow x \times y = 50 \rightarrow x \times 10 = 50 \rightarrow x = 5$

**2) Choice C is correct**

Two triangles $\Delta BAE$ and $\Delta BCD$ are similar. Then: $\frac{AE}{CD} = \frac{AB}{BC} \rightarrow \frac{4}{6} = \frac{x}{12} \rightarrow 48 - 4x = 6x \rightarrow$

$$10x = 48 \rightarrow x = 4.8$$

**3) Choice D is correct**

$$\frac{2}{5} \times 25 = \frac{50}{5} = 10$$

**4) Choice C is correct**

Use the area of rectangle formula (A = length × width). Let $A_1$ be the area of bigger rectangle and $A_2$ be the area of smaller rectangle. To find area of the shaded region subtract smaller rectangle from bigger rectangle. $A_1 - A_2 = (10ft \times 8ft) - (5ft \times 8ft) \Rightarrow A_1 - A_2 = 40ft$

**5) The answer is: $-64$**

Use PEMDAS (order of operation): $[3 \times (-14) - 48] - 14 + [3 \times 8] \div 2 =$

$$[-42 - 48] + 14 + 24 \div 2 = -90 + 14 + 12 = -64$$

**6) Choice A is correct**

To solve absolute values equations, write two equations. $2x - 6$ can equal positive 12, or negative 12. Therefore, $2x - 6 = 12 \Rightarrow 2x = 18 \Rightarrow x = 9$.

$2x - 6 = -12 \Rightarrow 2x = -12 + 6 = -6 \Rightarrow x = -3$.

Find the product of solutions: $-3 \times 9 = -27$

**7) Choice B is correct**

The equation of a line in slope intercept form is: $y = mx + b$. Solve for $y$. $3x - y = 6 \rightarrow$

$-y = -3x + 6$. Divide both sides by $(-1)$. Then: $-y = -3x + 6 \rightarrow y = 3x - 6$

The slope of this line is 3. The product of the slopes of two perpendicular lines is $-1$. Therefore, the slope of a line that is perpendicular to this line is: $m_1 \times m_2 = -1 \Rightarrow 3 \times m_2 = -1 \Rightarrow$

$$m_2 = \frac{-1}{3} = -\frac{1}{3}$$

**8) Choice C is correct**

Plug in the value of $x$ and $y$. $3(x - 2y) + (2 - x)^2$ when $x = 5$ and $y = -3$

$3(x - 2y) + (2 - x)^2 = 3(5 - 2(-3)) + (2 - 5)^2 = 3(5 + 6) + (-3)^2 = 33 + 9 = 42$

**9) The answer is 2.5**

First, use distribute property to simplify $-4(x + 2)$.     $-4(x + 2) = -4x - 8$

Now, combine like terms: $x - 4(x + 2) = -15.5 \rightarrow x - 4x - 8 = -15.5 \rightarrow -3x - 8 = -15.5$

Add 8 to both sides of the equation: $-3x - 8 + 8 = -15.5 + 8 \rightarrow -3x = -7.5$. Divide both sides by $-3$. Then: $-3x = -7.5 \rightarrow \frac{-3x}{-3} = \frac{-7.5}{-3} \rightarrow x = 2.5$

**10) Choice D is correct**

Solve for $x$. $x - 4 \leq 4x - 8 < 16 \Rightarrow$ (add 8 all sides) $-4 + 8 < 4x - 8 + 8 < 16 + 8 \Rightarrow$

$4 < 4x < 24 \Rightarrow$ (divide all sides by 4) $1 \leq x < 6$

$x$ is between 1 and 6. Choice D represents this inequality.

**11) Choice A is correct**

Simplify and combine like terms. $(6x^3 - 8x^2 + 2x^4) - (4x^2 - 2x^4 + 2x^3) \Rightarrow$
$(6x^3 - 8x^2 + 2x^4) - 4x^2 + 2x^4 - 2x^3 \Rightarrow 4x^4 + 4x^3 - 12x^2$

**12) Choice C is correct**

the population is increased by 15% and 20%. 15% increase changes the population to 115% of original population. For the second increase, multiply the result by 120%.

$(1.15) \times (1.20) = 1.38 = 138\%$. 38 percent of the population is increased after two years.

**13) Choice C is correct**

Three times of 24,000 is 72,000. One sixth of them cancelled their tickets.

One sixth of 72,000 equals 12,000 ($\frac{1}{6} \times 72,000 = 12,000$).

60,000 ($72000 - 12,000 = 60,000$) fans are attending this week

**14) The answer is 97.6**

The area of the square is 595.36. Therefore, the side of the square is square root of the area.

$\sqrt{595.36} = 24.4.$       Four times the side of the square is the perimeter: $4 \times 24.4 = 97.6$

**15) Choice C is correct**

average (mean) $= \frac{\text{sum of terms}}{\text{number of terms}} \Rightarrow 88 = \frac{\text{sum of terms}}{50} \Rightarrow sum = 88 \times 50 = 4,400$

The difference of 94 and 69 is 25. Therefore, 25 should be subtracted from the sum.

$4400 - 25 = 4,375$, mean $\frac{\text{sum of terms}}{\text{number of terms}} \Rightarrow mean = \frac{4,375}{50} = 87.5$

**16) Choice B is correct**

For sum of 5: $(1 \& 4)$ *and* $(4 \& 1), (2 \& 3)$ and $(3 \& 2)$, therefore we have 4 options.
For sum of 8: $(5 \& 3)$ *and* $(3 \& 5), (4 \& 4)$ and $(2 \& 6), (6 \& 2)$, we have 9 options. To get a sum of 5 or 8 for two dice: $4 + 5 = 9$
Since, we have $6 \times 6 = 36$ total number of options, the probability of getting a sum of 5 and 8 is 11 out of 36 or $\frac{9}{36} = \frac{1}{4}$

**17) The answer is 8.**

Use formula of rectangle prism volume. $V = (length)(width)(height) \Rightarrow$

$2000 = (25)(10)(height) \Rightarrow height = 2,000 \div 250 = 8$

**18) Choice C is correct**

To find the number of possible outfit combinations, multiply number of options for each factor:

$3 \times 5 \times 4 = 60$

**19) Choice A is correct**

In the stadium the ratio of home fans to visiting fans in a crowd is $5:7$. Therefore, total number of fans must be divisible by 12: $5 + 7 = 12$.
Let's review the choices:

☐A. 12,324:       $12,324 \div 12 = 1,027$

☐B. 42,326       $42,326 \div 12 = 3,527.166$

☐C. 44,566       $44,566 \div 12 = 3,713.833$

☐D. 66,812          $66,812 \div 12 = 5,567.66666$

Only choice A when divided by 12 results a whole number.

## 20) Choice B is correct

The diagonal of the square is 8. Let $x$ be the side.

Use Pythagorean Theorem: $a^2 + b^2 = c^2$

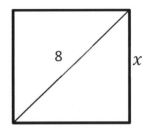

$x^2 + x^2 = 8^2 \Rightarrow 2x^2 = 8^2 \Rightarrow 2x^2 = 64 \Rightarrow x^2 = 32 \Rightarrow x = \sqrt{32}$

The area of the square is: $\sqrt{32} \times \sqrt{32} = 32$

## 21) Choice B is correct

$\text{Probability} = \dfrac{number\ of\ desired\ outcomes}{number\ of\ total\ outcomes} = \dfrac{18}{12+18+18+24} = \dfrac{18}{72} = \dfrac{1}{4}$

## 22) Choice A is correct

The width of the rectangle is twice its length. Let $x$ be the length. Then, $width = 2x$

Perimeter of the rectangle is $2\ (width + length)\ = 2(2x + x) = 60 \Rightarrow 6x = 60 \Rightarrow x = 10$

Length of the rectangle is 10 meters.

## 23) Choice D is correct

$\text{average} = \dfrac{\text{sum of terms}}{\text{number of terms}} \Rightarrow$ (average of 6 numbers) $12 = \dfrac{\text{sum of numbers}}{6} \Rightarrow$ sum of 6 numbers is $12 \times 6 = 72$

(average of 4 numbers) $10 = \dfrac{\text{sum of numbers}}{4} \Rightarrow$ sum of 4 numbers is $10 \times 4 = 40$

$sum\ of\ 6\ numbers - sum\ of\ 4\ numbers\ = sum\ of\ 2\ numbers,\ 72 - 40 = 32,$

$\text{average of 2 numbers} = \dfrac{32}{2} = 16$

## 24) Choice C is correct

Solving Systems of Equations by Elimination

Multiply the first equation by $(-2)$, then add it to the second equation.

$\begin{array}{l} -2(2x + 5y = 11) \\ \underline{4x - 2y = -14} \end{array} \Rightarrow \begin{array}{l} -4x - 10y = -22 \\ 4x - 2y = -14 \end{array} \Rightarrow -12y = -36 \Rightarrow y = 3$

Plug in the value of $y$ into one of the equations and solve for $x$.

$2x + 5(3) = 11 \Rightarrow 2x + 15 = 11 \Rightarrow 2x = -4 \Rightarrow x = -2$

## 25) Choice B is correct

The perimeter of the trapezoid is $36\ cm$. Therefore, the missing side (height) is $= 36 - 8 - 12 - 6 = 10$. Area of a trapezoid: $A = \frac{1}{2} \cdot h\ (b_1 + b_2) = \frac{1}{2}\ (10)\ (6 + 8) = 70$

## 26) Choice B is correct

The probability of choosing a Hearts is $\frac{13}{52} = \frac{1}{4}$

## 27) Choice D is correct

First, find the sum of five numbers.

$$\text{average} \ = \frac{\text{sum of terms}}{\text{number of terms}} \Rightarrow 25 = \frac{\text{sum of 5 numbers}}{5} \Rightarrow \text{sum of 5 numbers} = 25 \times 5\ = 125$$

The sum of 5 numbers is 125. If a sixth number that is greater than 42 is added to these numbers, then the sum of 6 numbers must be greater than 162. $125 + 42 = 167$

If the number was 42, then the average of the numbers is: $\text{average} = \frac{\text{sum of terms}}{\text{number of terms}}\ = \frac{167}{6} =$ 27.83. Since the number is bigger than 42. Then, the average of six numbers must be greater than 27.83. Choice D is greater than 27.83.

## 28) The answer is 28.

Let $x$ be the width of the rectangle. Use Pythagorean Theorem:

$$a^2 + b^2 = c^2$$

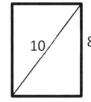

$$x^2 + 8^2 = 10^2\ \Rightarrow x^2 + 64 = 100\ \Rightarrow\ x^2 = 100 - 64\ = 36 \Rightarrow\ x\ = 6$$

Perimeter of the rectangle $=\ 2\ (length\ +\ width) = 2\ (8 + 6) = 2\ (14) = 28$

## 29) Choice C is correct

Th ratio of boy to girls is $4:7$. Therefore, there are 4 boys out of 11 students. To find the answer, first divide the total number of students by 11, then multiply the result by 4. $44 \div\ 11 = 4 \Rightarrow 4 \times 4\ = 16$. There are 16 boys and 28 $(44 - 16)$ girls. So, 12 more boys should be enrolled to make the ratio $1:1$

## 30) Choice A is correct

2,500 out of 55,000 equals to $\frac{2500}{55000} = \frac{25}{550} = \frac{1}{22}$

## 31) The answer is 60.

Jason needs an 75% average to pass for five exams. Therefore, the sum of 5 exams must be at lease $5 \times 75 = 375$. The sum of 4 exams is: $68 + 72 + 85 +\ 90 = 315$.

The minimum score Jason can earn on his fifth and final test to pass is: $375 - 315 = 60$

**32) Choice D is correct**

Isolate and solve for $x$. $\frac{2}{3}x + \frac{1}{6} = \frac{1}{3} \Rightarrow \frac{2}{3}x = \frac{1}{3} - \frac{1}{6} = \frac{1}{6} \Rightarrow \frac{2}{3}x = \frac{1}{6}$

Multiply both sides by the reciprocal of the coefficient of $x$. $\left(\frac{3}{2}\right)\frac{2}{3}x = \frac{1}{6}\left(\frac{3}{2}\right) \Rightarrow x = \frac{3}{12} = \frac{1}{4}$

**33) Choice B is correct**

Use simple interest formula: $I = prt$ (I = interest, p = principal, r = rate, t = time)

$I = (12000)(0.035)(2) = 840$

**34) Choice D is correct**

Simplify. $6x^2y^3(2x^2y)^3 = 6x^2y^3(8x^6y^3) = 48x^8y^6$

**35) Choice C is correct**

Surface Area of a cylinder $= 2\pi r \, (r + h)$, The radius of the cylinder is 3 ($6 \div 2$) inches and its height is 8 inches. Therefore, Surface Area of a cylinder $= 2\pi \, (3) \, (3 + 8) \, = 66\,\pi$

**36) The answer is 170.**

Use the information provided in the question to draw the shape.

Use Pythagorean Theorem: $a^2 + b^2 = c^2$

$80^2 + 150^2 = c^2 \Rightarrow 6400 + 22500 = c^2 \Rightarrow 28900 = c^2 \Rightarrow c = 170$

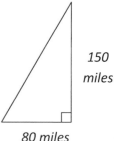

*150 miles*

*80 miles*

**37) Choice B is correct**

Plug in 104 for $F$ and then solve for $C$. $C = \frac{5}{9}\,(F - 32) \Rightarrow C = \frac{5}{9}\,(104 - 32) \Rightarrow$

$C = \frac{5}{9}\,(72) = 40$

**38) Choice D is correct**

Let $x$ be all expenses, then $\frac{22}{100}x = \$660 \rightarrow x = \frac{100 \times \$660}{22} = \$3,000$. He spent for his rent: $\frac{27}{100} \times \$3,000 = \$810$

**39) Choice A is correct**

First, find the number. Let $x$ be the number. Write the equation and solve for $x$.

150% of a number is 75, then: $1.5 \times x = 75 \Rightarrow x = 75 \div 1.5 = 50$

90% of 50 is: $\quad\quad 0.9 \times 50 = 45$

**40) Choice A is correct**

Let $x$ be the number of new shoes the team can purchase. Therefore, the team can purchase $120\ x$. The team had $20,000 and spent $14,000. Now the team can spend on new shoes $6,000 at most. Now, write the inequality: $120x + 14,000 \leq 20,000$

# STAAR Mathematics Practice Test 2

## Answers and Explanations

**1) Choice C is correct**

$x$ is directly proportional to the square of $y$. Then: $x = cy^2 \rightarrow 12 = c(2)^2 \rightarrow 12 = 4c \rightarrow c = \frac{12}{4} = 3$. The relationship between $x$ and $y$ is: $x = 3y^2, x = 75$

$$75 = 3y^2 \rightarrow y^2 = \frac{75}{3} = 25 \rightarrow y = 5$$

**2) Choice D is correct**

The amount of money that jack earns for one hour: $\frac{\$616}{44} = \$14$

Number of additional hours that he work to make enough money is: $\quad \frac{\$826-\$616}{1.5\times\$14} = 10$

Number of total hours is: $\quad 44 + 10 = 54$

**3) Choice B is correct**

Let's find the mean (average), mode and median of the number of cities for each type of pollution. Number of cities for each type of pollution: 6, 3, 4, 9, 8

$$average\ (mean) = \frac{sum\ of\ terms}{number\ of\ terms} = \frac{6+3+4+9+8}{5} = \frac{30}{5} = 6$$

Median is the number in the middle. To find median, first list numbers in order from smallest to largest. 3, 4, 6, 8, 9. Median of the data is 6. Mode is the number which appears most often in a set of numbers. Therefore, there is no mode in the set of numbers. Median = Mean, then,

$a = c$

**4) Choice A is correct**

Percent of cities in the type of pollution A: $\frac{6}{10} \times 100 = 60\%$

Percent of cities in the type of pollution C: $\frac{4}{10} \times 100 = 40\%$

Percent of cities in the type of pollution E: $\frac{9}{10} \times 100 = 90\%$

**5) Choice A is correct**

Let the number of cities should be added to type of pollutions B be $x$. Then:

$$\frac{x+3}{8} = 0.625 \rightarrow x + 3 = 8 \times 0.625 \rightarrow x + 3 = 5 \rightarrow x = 2$$

**6) Choice A is correct**

$AB = 12$      And      $AC = 5. BC = \sqrt{12^2 + 5^2} = \sqrt{144 + 25} = \sqrt{169} = 13$

Perimeter $= 5 + 12 + 13 = 30.$      Area $= \frac{5 \times 12}{2} = 5 \times 6 = 30$

In this case, the ratio of the perimeter of the triangle to its area is: $\frac{30}{30} = 1$

If the sides AB and AC become twice longer, then: $AB = 24$      And      $AC = 10$

$BC = \sqrt{24^2 + 10^2} = \sqrt{576 + 100} = \sqrt{676} = 26.$ Perimeter $= 26 + 24 + 10 = 60$

Area $= \frac{10 \times 24}{2} = 10 \times 12 = 120$

In this case the ratio of the perimeter of the triangle to its area is: $\frac{60}{120} = \frac{1}{2}$

**7) Choice B is correct**

In scientific notation all numbers are written in the form of: $m \times 10^n$, where $m$ is between 1 and 10. To find an equivalent value of 0.000 000 000 000 042 121, move the decimal point to the right so that you have a number that is between 1 and 10.  Then: 4.2121

Now, determine how many places the decimal moved in step 1, then put it as the power of 10. We moved the decimal point 14 places. Then: $10^{-1}$   → When the decimal moved to the right, the exponent is negative. Then: $0.000\ 000\ 000\ 000\ 042\ 121 = 4.2121 \times 10^{-14}$

**8) Choice D is correct**

To find the discount, multiply the number by $(100\% - rate\ of\ discount)$.

Therefore, for the first discount we get: $(200)(100\% - 15\%) = (200)(0.85) = 170$

For the next 15% discount: $(200)(0.85)(0.85)$

## 9) Choice B is correct

Plug in each pair of number in the equation:

- A.  $(2, 1)$:     $2(2) + 4(1) = 8$
- B.  $(-1, 3)$:    $2(-1) + 4(3) = 10$
- C.  $(-2, 2)$:    $2(-2) + 4(2) = 4$
- D.  $(2, 2)$:     $2(2) + 4(2) = 12$

Only choice B is correct.

## 10) The answer is: $-30$

Use PEMDAS (order of operation): $5 + 8 \times (-2) - [4 + 22 \times 5] \div 6 = 5 + 8 \times (-2) - [4 + 110] \div 6 = 5 + 8 \times (-2) - [114] \div 6 = 5 + (-16) - 19 = 5 + (-16) - 19 = -11 - 19 = -30$

## 11) Choice B is correct.

To find the area of the shaded region subtract smaller circle from bigger circle.

$S_{bigger} - S_{smaller} = \pi (r_{bigger})^2 - \pi (r_{smaller})^2 \Rightarrow S_{bigger} - S_{smaller} = \pi (6)^2 - \pi (4)^2$

$\Rightarrow 36\pi - 16\pi = 20\pi$

## 12) Choice C is correct

85% of 40 is: $85\% \ of \ 40 = 0.85 \times 40 = 34$. So, the student solves 34 questions correctly.

## 13) Choice C is correct

Write the equation and solve for B: $0.60 \ A = 0.30 \ B$, divide both sides by 0.30, then:

$\frac{0.60}{0.30} \ A = B$, therefore: $B = 2 \ A$, and $B$ is 2 times of $A$ or it's 200% of $A$.

## 14) The answer is 90.

To find the number of possible outfit combinations, multiply number of options for each factor:

$6 \times 3 \times 5 = 90$

## 15) Choice D is correct

The relationship among all sides of special right triangle

$30° - 60° - 90°$ is provided in this triangle:

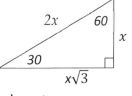

In this triangle, the opposite side of $30°$ angle is half of the hypotenuse.

Draw the shape for this question:

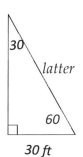

The latter is the hypotenuse. Therefore, the latter is $60\ ft$.

### 16) Choice C is correct

Let $x$ be the number. Write the equation and solve for $x$. $(24 - x) \div x = 3$. Multiply both sides by $x$. $(24 - x) = 3x$, then add x both sides. $24 = 4x$, now divide both sides by 4. $x = 6$

### 17) Choice B is correct

The sum of supplement angles is 180. Let $x$ be that angle. Therefore, $x + 5x = 180$. $6 = 180$, divide both sides by 6: $x = 30$

### 18) Choice C is correct

The average speed of john is: $150 \div 6 = 25\ km,$ The average speed of Alice is: $180 \div 4 = 45\ km$. Write the ratio and simplify. $25 : 45 \Rightarrow 5 : 9$

### 19) The answer is $-5$.

Solving Systems of Equations by Elimination

$$3x - 4y = -40$$
$$\underline{-x + 2y = 10}$$    Multiply the second equation by 3, then add it to the first equation.

$$\frac{3x - 4y = -40}{3(-x + 2y = 10)} \Rightarrow \frac{3x - 4y = -40}{-3x + 6y = 30)} \Rightarrow 2y = -10 \Rightarrow y = -5$$

### 20) Choice C is correct

Add the first 5 numbers. $40 + 45 + 50 + 35 + 55 = 225$. To find the distance traveled in the next 5 hours, multiply the average by number of hours. $Distance\ =\ Average\ \times\ Rate\ =\ 50 \times 5\ =\ 250.$    Add both numbers. $250 + 225 = 475$

### 21) Choice C is correct

Use distance formula: $Distance\ =\ Rate \times time\ \Rightarrow\ 420\ =\ 50\ \times\ T$, divide both sides by 50. $420 \div 50 = T \Rightarrow T\ =\ 8.4\ hours.$

Change hours to minutes for the decimal part. $0.4\ hours\ =\ 0.4\ \times\ 60\ =\ 24\ minutes.$

### 22) Choice D is correct

Use Pythagorean Theorem: $a^2 + b^2 = c^2, 6^2\ +\ 8^2\ = c^2\ \Rightarrow\ 100\ =\ c^2\ \Rightarrow\ c\ =\ 10$

### 23) The answer is $240$.

Th ratio of boy to girls is $2 : 3$. Therefore, there are 2 boys out of 5 students. To find the answer, first divide the total number of students by 5, then multiply the result by 2.

$600 \div 5 = 120 \Rightarrow 120 \times 2 = 240$

**24) The answer is 130.**

The perimeter of the trapezoid is 54.

Therefore, the missing side (height) is $= 54 - 18 - 12 - 14 = 10$

Area of a trapezoid: $A = \frac{1}{2} h (b_1 + b_2) = \frac{1}{2}(10)(12 + 14) = 130$

**25) Choice C is correct**

Let $x$ be the number. Write the equation and solve for $x$.

$\frac{2}{3} \times 18 = \frac{2}{5} \cdot x \Rightarrow \frac{2 \times 18}{3} = \frac{2x}{5}$, use cross multiplication to solve for $x$.

$5 \times 36 = 2x \times 3 \Rightarrow 180 = 6x \Rightarrow x = 30$

**26) Choice B is correct**

To find the discount, multiply the number by $(100\% - rate\ of\ discount)$.

Therefore, for the first discount we get: $(D)(100\% - 20\%) = (D)(0.80) = 0.80\ D$

For increase of 10%: $(0.80\ D)(100\% + 10\%) = (0.80D)(1.10) = 0.88\ D = 88\%\ of\ D$

**27) Choice A is correct**

Let $x$ be the number of years. Therefore, \$2,000 per year equals $2000x$. starting from \$24,000 annual salary means you should add that amount to $2000x$. Income more than that is:

$I > 2000x + 24000$

**28) Choice C is correct**

The question is this: 1.75 is what percent of 1.25? Use percent formula:

$\text{part} = \frac{\text{percent}}{100} \times \text{whole} \Rightarrow 1.75 = \frac{percent}{100} \times 1.25 \Rightarrow 1.75 = \frac{percent \times 1.25}{100} \Rightarrow$

$175 = percent \times 1.25 \Rightarrow percent = \frac{175}{1.25} = 140$

**29) Choice B is correct**

Use the information provided in the question to draw the shape.

Use Pythagorean Theorem: $a^2 + b^2 = c^2$

$40^2 + 30^2 = c^2 \Rightarrow 1600 + 900 = c^2 \Rightarrow 2500 = c^2 \Rightarrow c = 50$

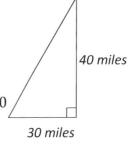

40 miles

30 miles

**30) Choice B is correct**

The question is this: 529.72 is what percent of 646? Use percent formula:

$$part = \frac{percent}{100} \times whole. \qquad 529.72 = \frac{percent}{100} \times 646 \Rightarrow 529.72 = \frac{percent \times 646}{100} \Rightarrow$$

$$529.72 = percent \times 646 \Rightarrow percent = \frac{529.72}{646} = 82$$

529.72 is 82% of 646. Therefore, the discount is: $100\% - 82\% = 18\%$

### 31) Choice D is correct

If 17 balls are removed from the bag at random, there will be one ball in the bag. The probability of choosing a brown ball is 1 out of 18. Therefore, the probability of not choosing a brown ball is 17 out of 18 and the probability of having not a brown ball after removing 17 balls is the same.

### 32) Choice B is correct

Let $x$ be the smallest number. Then, these are the numbers: $x, x + 1, x + 2, x + 3, x + 4$

$$average = \frac{sum\ of\ terms}{number\ of\ terms} \Rightarrow 38 = \frac{x+(x+1)+(x+2)+(x+3)+(x+4)}{5} \Rightarrow 38 = \frac{5x+10}{5} \Rightarrow$$

$$190 = 5x + 10 \Rightarrow 180 = 5x \Rightarrow x = 36$$

### 33) Choice C is correct

The weight of 12.2 meters of this rope is: $12.2 \times 600\ g = 7320\ g$

$1\ kg = 1000\ g$, therefore, $7320\ g \div 1000 = 7.32\ kg$

### 34) Choice C is correct

4% of the volume of the solution is alcohol. Let $x$ be the volume of the solution.

Then: $4\%\ of\ x = 32\ ml \Rightarrow 0.04\ x = 32 \Rightarrow x = 32 \div 0.04 = 800$

### 35) Choice B is correct

$average = \frac{sum\ of\ terms}{number\ of\ terms}$. The sum of the weight of all girls is: $23 \times 60 = 1,380\ kg$, The sum of the weight of all boys is: $32 \times 62 = 1984\ kg$. The sum of the weight of all students is: $1,380 + 1,984 = 3,364\ kg.$ $\qquad average = \frac{3364}{55} = 61.16$

### 36) Choice D is correct

Let $x$ be the original price. If the price of a laptop is decreased by 20% to $360, then:

$80\%\ of\ x = 360 \Rightarrow 0.80x = 360 \Rightarrow x = 360 \div 0.80 = 450$

### 37) The answer is $678.24$.

Surface Area of a cylinder $= 2\pi r(r + h)$, The radius of the cylinder is 6 inches and its height is 12 inches. $\pi$ is about 3.14. Then: Surface Area of a cylinder $= 2(\pi)(6)(6 + 12) = 216\ \pi = 678.24$

**38) The answer is 12.**

$$average = \frac{sum\ of\ terms}{number\ of\ terms} \Rightarrow 15 = \frac{13 + 15 + 20 + x}{4} \Rightarrow 60 = 48 + x \Rightarrow x = 12$$

**39) Choice D is correct**

The equation of a line is in the form of $y = mx + b$, where $m$ is the slope of the line and $b$ is the $y - intercept$ of the line. Two points $(1, 2)$ and $(-1, 6)$ are on line $A$. Therefore, the slope of the line $A$ is: $slope\ of\ line\ A = \frac{y_2 - y_1}{x_2 - x_1} = \frac{6-2}{-1-1} = \frac{4}{-2} = -2$

The slope of line $A$ is $-2$. Thus, the formula of the line $A$ is: $y = mx + b = -2x + b$, choose a point and plug in the values of $x$ and $y$ in the equation to solve for $b$. Let's choose point $(1, 2)$. Then: $y = -2x + b \to 2 = -2(1) + b \to b = 2 + 2 = 4$. The equation of line $A$ is: $y = -2x + 4$

Now, let's review the choices provided:

A. $(-1, 2)$      $y = -2x + 4 \to 2 = -2(-1) + 4 = 6$      This is not true.

B. $(5, 7)$      $y = -2x + 4 \to 7 = -2(5) + 4 = -6$      This is not true.

C. $(3, 4)$      $y = -2x + 4 \to 4 = -2(3) + 4 = -2$      This is not true.

D. $(3, -2)$      $y = -2x + 4 \to -2 = -2(3) + 4 = -2$      This is true!

**40) Choice C is correct**

Use simple interest formula: $I = prt$ ($I = interest, p = principal, r = rate, t = time$)

$$I = (9,000)(0.045)(5) = 2,025$$

# STAAR Mathematics Practice Test 3

## Answers and Explanations

**1)  Choice D is correct**

The capacity of a red box is 20% bigger than the capacity of a blue box and it can hold 30 books. Therefore, we want to find a number that 20% bigger than that number is 30. Let $x$ be that number. Then:  $1.20 \times x = 30$, Divide both sides of the equation by 1.2. Then: $x = \frac{30}{1.20} = 25$

**2)  Choice C is correct**

The smallest number is $-15$. To find the largest possible value of one of the other five integers, we need to choose the smallest possible integers for four of them. Let $x$ be the largest number. Then: $-70 = (-15) + (-14) + (-13) + (-12) + (-11) + x \to -70 = -65 + x$

$$\to x = -70 + 65 = -5$$

**3)  The answer is: $-122$**

Use PEMDAS (order of operation):

$[6 \times (-24) + 8] - (-4) + [4 \times 5] \div 2 = [-144 + 8] - (-4) + [20] \div 2 =$

$[-144 + 8] - (-4) + 10 = [-136] - (-4) + 10 = [-136] + 4 + 10 = -122$

**4)  Choice D is correct**

Use FOIL method. $(2x + 2y)(2x - y) = 4x^2 - 2xy + 4xy - 2y^2 = 4x^2 + 2xy - 2y^2$

**5)  Choice D is correct**

To solve absolute values equations, write two equations. $x - 10$ could be positive 3, or negative 3. Therefore, $x - 10 = 3 \Rightarrow x = 13.$          $x - 10 = -3 \Rightarrow x = 7.$

Find the product of solutions: $7 \times 13 = 91$

**6)  Choice B is correct**

The equation of a line in slope intercept form is: $y = \mathrm{m}x + b$. Solve for $y$.

$4x - 2y = 12 \Rightarrow -2y = 12 - 4x \Rightarrow y = (12 - 4x) \div (-2) \Rightarrow y = 2x - 6$. The slope of this line is 2. The product of the slopes of two perpendicular lines is $-1$. Therefore, the slope of a line that is perpendicular to this line is: $m_1 \times m_2 = -1 \Rightarrow 2 \times m_2 = -1 \Rightarrow m_2 = \frac{-1}{2} = -\frac{1}{2}$

**7)  Choice A is correct**

Plug in the value of $x$ and $y$. $x = 3$ and $y = -2$

$5(x + 2y) + (2 - x)^2 = 5(3 + 2(-2)) + (2 - 3)^2 = 5(3 - 4) + (-1)^2 = -5 + 1 = -4$

**8)  Choice D is correct**

The distance between Bob and Mike is 12 miles. Bob running at 6.5 miles per hour and Mike is running at the speed of 8 miles per hour. Therefore, every hour the distance is 1.5 miles less. $12 \div 1.5 = 8$

**9)  Choice D is correct**

The failing rate is 11 out of 44 or $\frac{11}{44}$. Change the fraction to percent: $\frac{11}{44} \times 100\% = 25\%$

25 percent of students failed. Therefore, 75 percent of students passed the exam.

**10) Choice D is correct**

Solve for $x$. $-1 \le 2x - 3 < 1 \Rightarrow$ (add 3 all sides) $-1 + 3 \le 2x - 3 + 3 < 1 + 3 \Rightarrow$

$2 \leq 2x < 4 \Rightarrow$ (divide all sides by 2) $1 \leq x < 2$.     $x$ is between 1 and 2. Choice D represents this inequality.

## 11) The answer is 60.

Let $x$ be the width of the rectangle. Use Pythagorean Theorem: $a^2 + b^2 = c^2$

$x^2 + 5^2 = 13^2 \Rightarrow x^2 + 25 = 169 \Rightarrow x^2 = 169 - 25 = 144 \Rightarrow x = 12$

Area of the rectangle $= \ length \times width = 5 \times 12 = 60$

## 12) Choice B is correct

The perimeter of the trapezoid is $36\ cm$. Therefore, the missing side (height) is

$40 - 8 - 12 - 6 = 14$. Area of a trapezoid: $A\ =\ \frac{1}{2}\ h\ (b_1\ +\ b_2) = \frac{1}{2}\ (14)(6 + 8) = 98$

## 13) Choice B is correct

The probability of choosing a Club is $\frac{13}{52} = \frac{1}{4}$

## 14) Choice B is correct

$$average\ (mean) = \frac{sum\ of\ terms}{number\ of\ terms} \Rightarrow 80 = \frac{sum\ of\ terms}{50} \Rightarrow sum = 80 \times 50 = 4,000$$

The difference of 94 and 69 is 25. Therefore, 25 should be subtracted from the sum.

$4000 - 25 = 3,975.\ \ mean\ = \frac{sum\ of\ terms}{number\ of\ terms} \Rightarrow mean = \frac{3,975}{50} = 79.5$

## 15) Choice B is correct

To get a sum of 6 for two dice, we can receive $(1,5),(5,1),(2,4),(4,2),(3,3)$. So, we have 5 options. To get a sum of 9, we can receive $(6,3),(3,6),(4,5),(5,4)$. So, we have 4 options. Since, we have $6 \times 6\ = 36$ total options, the probability of getting a sum of 6 and 9 is 9 $(4 + 5)$ out of 36 or $\frac{9}{36} = \frac{1}{4}$

## 16) The answer is 10.

Use formula of rectangle prism volume. $V\ =\ (length)(width)(height) \Rightarrow$

$$2500 = (25)(10)(height) \Rightarrow height = 2,500 \div 250 = 10$$

## 17) Choice C is correct

To find the number of possible outfit combinations, multiply number of options for each factor:

$3 \times 5 \times 6\ = 90$

**18) Choice C is correct**

$4 \div \dfrac{1}{3} = 12$

**19) Choice A is correct**

The diagonal of the square is 4. Let $x$ be the side. Use Pythagorean Theorem: $a^2 + b^2 = c^2$

$x^2 + x^2 = 4^2 \Rightarrow 2x^2 = 4^2 \Rightarrow 2x^2 = 16 \Rightarrow x^2 = 8 \Rightarrow x = \sqrt{8}$

The area of the square is: $\sqrt{8} \times \sqrt{8} = 8$

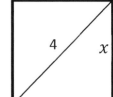

**20) Choice C is correct**

$\text{Probability} = \dfrac{number\ of\ desired\ outcomes}{number\ of\ total\ outcomes} = \dfrac{10}{15 + 10 + 10 + 25} = \dfrac{10}{60} = \dfrac{1}{6}$

**21) Choice A is correct**

Volume of the cube is less than $64\ m^3$. Use the formula of volume of cubes.

$volume = (one\ side)^3 \Rightarrow 64 > \Rightarrow 64 > (one\ side)^3$. Find the cube root of both sides. Then: $4 > one\ side$. The side of the cube is less than 4. Only choice A is less than 4.

**22) Choice A is correct**

The width of the rectangle is twice its length. Let $x$ be the length. Then, $width = 2x$

Perimeter of the rectangle is $2\ (width + length) = 2(2x + x) = 72 \Rightarrow 6x = 72 \Rightarrow$

$x = 12$. Length of the rectangle is 12 meters.

**23) Choice D is correct**

$average = \dfrac{\text{sum of terms}}{\text{number of terms}} \Rightarrow$ (average of 6 numbers) $10 = \dfrac{\text{sum of numbers}}{6} \Rightarrow$ sum of 6 numbers is $10 \times 6 = 60$

(average of 4 numbers) $7 = \dfrac{\text{sum of numbers}}{4} \Rightarrow$ sum of 4 numbers is $7 \times 4 = 28$

$sum\ of\ 6\ numbers - sum\ of\ 4\ numbers = sum\ of\ 2\ numbers$

$60 - 28 = 32.$     Average of 2 numbers $= \dfrac{32}{2} = 16$

**24) Choice C is correct**

Solving Systems of Equations by Elimination

Multiply the first equation by $(-2)$, then add it to the second equation.

$$-2(2x + 5y = 11) \Rightarrow \frac{-4x - 10y = -22}{4x - 2y = -26} \Rightarrow -12y = -48 \Rightarrow y = 4$$

Plug in the value of $y$ into one of the equations and solve for $x$.

$$2x + 5(4) = 11 \Rightarrow 2x + 20 = 11 \Rightarrow 2x = -9 \Rightarrow x = -4.5$$

### 25) Choice D is correct

Area of the circle is less than $81\pi \ ft^2$. Use the formula of areas of circles. $Area = \pi r^2 \Rightarrow$ $81\pi > \pi r^2 \Rightarrow 81 > r^2 \Rightarrow r < 9$. Radius of the circle is less than $9 \ ft$. Therefore, the diameter of the circle is less than $18 \ ft$. Only choice D is less than $18 ft$.

### 26) Choice D is correct

Th ratio of boy to girls is $4 : 7$. Therefore, there are 4 boys out of 11 students. To find the answer, first divide the total number of students by 11, then multiply the result by 4. $55 \div 11 = 5 \Rightarrow$ $5 \times 4 = 20$. There are 20 boys and $35 \ (55 - 20)$ girls. So, 15 more boys should be enrolled to make the ratio $1 : 1$

### 27) Choice A is correct

Let $x$ be the number of new shoes the team can purchase. Therefore, the team can purchase $120 \ x$. The team had $20,000 and spent $10000. Now the team can spend on new shoes $10,000 at most. Now, write the inequality: $120x + 10,000 \leq 20,000$

### 28) The answer is 35.

Jason needs an 70% average to pass for five exams. Therefore, the sum of 5 exams must be at lease $5 \times 70 = 350$. The sum of 4 exams is: $68 + 72 + 85 + 90 = 315$.

The minimum score Jason can earn on his fifth and final test to pass is: $350 - 315 = 35$

### 29) Choice B is correct

Isolate and solve for $x$. $\frac{2}{3}x + \frac{1}{6} = \frac{1}{2} \Rightarrow \frac{2}{3}x = \frac{1}{2} - \frac{1}{6} = \frac{1}{3} \Rightarrow \frac{2}{3}x = \frac{1}{3}$

Multiply both sides by the reciprocal of the coefficient of $x$. $(\frac{3}{2})\frac{2}{3}x = \frac{1}{3}(\frac{3}{2}) \Rightarrow x = \frac{3}{6} = \frac{1}{2}$

### 30) Choice B is correct

Use simple interest formula: $I = prt$ (I = interest, p = principal, r = rate, t = time)

$$I = (14000)(0.035)(2) = 980$$

**31) Choice D is correct**

Simplify. $5x^2y^3(2x^2y)^3 = 5x^2y^3(8x^6y^3) = 40x^8y^6$

**32) Choice C is correct**

Surface Area of a cylinder $= 2\pi r\,(r + h)$, the radius of the cylinder is 2 (4 ÷ 2) inches and its height is 8 inches. Therefore, Surface Area of a cylinder $= 2\pi\,(2)\,(2 + 8)\, = 40\,\pi$

**33) Choice D is correct**

First, find the sum of four numbers. average $= \dfrac{\text{sum of terms}}{\text{number of terms}} \Rightarrow 48 = \dfrac{\text{sum of 4 numbers}}{4} \Rightarrow$ sum of 4 numbers $= 48 \times 4 = 192$. The sum of 4 numbers is 192. If a fifth number that is greater than 65 is added to these numbers, then the sum of 5 numbers must be greater than $192 + 65 = 257$. If the number was 65, then the average of the numbers is:

average $= \dfrac{256}{5} = 51.4$. Since the number is bigger than 65. Then, the average of five numbers must be greater than 51.4. Choice D is greater than 51.4

**34) The answer is 130.**

Use the information provided in the question to draw the shape.

Use Pythagorean Theorem: $a^2 + b^2 = c^2$

$50^2 + 120^2 = c^2 \Rightarrow 2500 + 14400 = c^2 \Rightarrow 16900 = c^2 \Rightarrow c = 130$

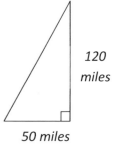

*120 miles*

*50 miles*

**35) Choice D is correct**

Plug in 140 for $F$ and then solve for $C$. $C = \dfrac{5}{9}\,(F - 32) \Rightarrow C = \dfrac{5}{9}\,(140 - 32) \Rightarrow$

$C = \dfrac{5}{9}(108) = 60$

**36) Choice A is correct**

First, find the number. Let $x$ be the number. Write the equation and solve for $x$. 150% of a number is 75, then: $1.5 \times x = 75 \Rightarrow x = 75 \div 1.5 = 50$. 80% of 50 is: $0.8 \times 50 = 40$

**37) Choice A is correct**

Simplify and combine like terms. $(5x^3 - 8x^2 + 2x^4) - (4x^2 - 2x^4 + 2x^3) \Rightarrow$
$(5x^3 - 8x^2 + 2x^4) - 4x^2 + 2x^4 - 2x^3 \Rightarrow 4x^4 + 3x^3 - 12x^2$

**38) Choice B is correct**

the population is increased by 10% and 20%. 10% increase changes the population to 110% of original population. For the second increase, multiply the result by 120%.

$(1.10) \times (1.20) = 1.32 = 132\%$. 32 percent of the population is increased after two years.

**39) Choice C is correct**

Three times of 25,000 is 75,000. One sixth of them cancelled their tickets.

One sixth of 75,000 equals 12,500 ($\frac{1}{6} \times 72,000 = 12,500$). 62,500 ($75,000 - 12,500 = 62,500$) fans are attending this week

**40) Choice B is correct.**

A linear equation is a relationship between two variables, $x$ and $y$, and can be written in the form of $y = mx + b$ . A non-proportional linear relationship takes on the form $y = mx + b$, where $b \neq 0$ and its graph is a line that does not cross through the origin. Only in graph B, the line does not pass through the origin

# STAAR Mathematics Practice Test 4

## Answers and Explanations

**1)  Choice D is correct**

The amount of money for $x$ bookshelf is:        $100x$

Then, the total cost of all bookshelves is equal to:    $100x + 800$

The total cost, in dollar, per bookshelf is: $\frac{Total\ cost}{number\ of\ items} = \frac{100x+800}{x}$

**2)  Choice C is correct**

$\sqrt{x} = 4 \rightarrow x = 16$. Then; $\sqrt{x} - 7 = \sqrt{16} - 7 = 4 - 7 = -3$ and $\sqrt{x - 7} = \sqrt{16 - 7} = \sqrt{9} = 3$

Then: $\left(\sqrt{x - 7}\right) + \left(\sqrt{x} - 7\right) = 3 + (-3) = 0$

**3)  Choice B is correct**

The angles on a straight line add up to 180 degrees. Then:

$x + 25 + y + 2x + y = 180$

Then, $3x + 2y = 180 - 25 \rightarrow 3(35) + 2y = 155$

$\rightarrow 2y = 155 - 105 = 50 \rightarrow y = 25$

**4)  Choice A is correct**

$|-12 - 5| - |-8 + 2| = |-17| - |-6| = 17 - 6 = 11$

**5) Choice B is correct**

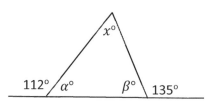

$\alpha = 180° - 112° = 68°$

$\beta = 180° - 135° = 45°$

$x + \alpha + \beta = 180° \rightarrow x = 180° - 68° - 45° = 67°$

**6) Choice D is correct**

A. $f(x) = x^2 - 5$     if     $x = 1 \rightarrow f(1) = (1)^2 - 5 = 1 - 5 = -4 \neq 5$

B. $f(x) = x^2 - 1$     if     $x = 1 \rightarrow f(1) = (1)^2 - 1 = 1 - 1 = 0 \neq 5$

C. $f(x) = \sqrt{x + 2}$     if     $x = 1 \rightarrow f(1) = \sqrt{1 + 2} = \sqrt{3} \neq 5$

D. $f(x) = \sqrt{x} + 4$     if     $x = 1 \rightarrow f(1) = \sqrt{1} + 4 = 5$

**7) Choice D is correct**

$3x - 5 = 8.5 \rightarrow 3x = 8.5 + 5 = 13.5 \rightarrow x = \frac{13.5}{3} = 4.5$

Then; $5x + 3 = 5\,(4.5) + 3 = 22.5 + 3 = 25.5$

**8) Choice C is correct**

First draw an isosceles triangle. Remember that two sides of the triangle are equal.

Let put $a$ for the legs. Then:

Isosceles right triangle

$a = 6 \Rightarrow$ area of the triangle is $= \frac{1}{2}\,(6 \times 6) = \frac{36}{2} = 18\ cm^2$

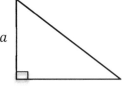

**9) Choice D is correct**

To find the discount, multiply the number by $(100\% - rate\ of\ discount)$.

Therefore, for the first discount we get: $(500)\,(100\% - 25\%) = (500)\,(0.75)$

For the next 15% discount: $(500)\,(0.75)\,(0.85)$

**10) Choice B is correct**

Plug in each pair of numbers in the equation: $3x + 5y = 7$

    A.  $(2, 1)$:      $3\,(2) + 5\,(1) = 11$
    B.  $(-1, 2)$:     $3(-1) + 5(2) = 7$
    C.  $(-2, 2)$:     $3(-2) + 5(2) = 4$
    D.  $(2, 2)$:      $3(2) + 5(2) = 16$

Choice B is correct.

**11) The answer is 24.**

$\text{average} = \dfrac{\text{sum of terms}}{\text{number of terms}} \Rightarrow 18 = \dfrac{13+15+20+x}{4} \Rightarrow 72 = 48 + x \Rightarrow x = 24$

**12) Choice C is correct**

Let $x$ be the number. Write the equation and solve for $x$. $(32 - x) \div x = 3$

Multiply both sides by $x$. $(32 - x) = 3x$, then add $x$ both sides. $32 = 4x$, now divide both sides by 4. $x = 8$

**13) Choice A is correct**

The sum of supplement angles is 180. Let $x$ be that angle. Therefore, $x + 9x = 180$

$10x = 180$, divide both sides by 10: $x = 18$

**14) Choice C is correct**

The average speed of john is: $140 \div 7 = 20 \; km$, The average speed of Alice is:

$180 \div 4 = 45 \; km$, Write the ratio and simplify. $20 : 45 = 4 : 9$

**15) Choice D is correct**

Use Pythagorean Theorem: $a^2 + b^2 = c^2$

$9^2 + 12^2 = c^2 \Rightarrow 81 + 144 = c^2 \Rightarrow 225 = c^2 \Rightarrow c = 15$

**16) Choice A is correct**

Area of the circle is less than $16\,\pi$. Use the formula of areas of circles.

$Area = \pi r^2 \Rightarrow 64\,\pi > \pi r^2 \Rightarrow 64 > r^2 \Rightarrow r < 8$

Radius of the circle is less than 8. Let's put 8 for the radius. Now, use the circumference formula: $Circumference = 2\pi r = 2\pi\,(8) = 16\,\pi$

Since the radius of the circle is less than 8. Then, the circumference of the circle must be less than $16\,\pi$. Only choice A is less than $16\,\pi$.

**17) The answer is 7.**

Solving Systems of Equations by Elimination

$\begin{array}{l} 3x - 4y = -16 \\ -x + 2y = 10 \end{array}$  Multiply the second equation by 3, then add it to the first equation.

$\begin{array}{l} 3x - 4y = -16 \\ 3(-x + 2y = 10) \end{array} \Rightarrow \begin{array}{l} 3x - 4y = -16 \\ -3x + 6y = 30) \end{array} \Rightarrow 2y = 14 \Rightarrow y = 7$

**18) Choice C is correct**

Use this formula: Percent of Change: $\dfrac{\text{New Value} - \text{Old Value}}{Old\ Value} \times 100\%$

$\dfrac{28,000 - 1\ ,200}{28,000} \times 100\% = -35\%$. The negative sign means that the price decreased.

**19) Choice D is correct**

If the length of the box is 36, then the width of the box is one third of it, 12, and the height of the box is 4 (one third of the width). The volume of the box is: $V = lwh = (36)(12)(4) = 1,728$

**20) The answer is 120.**

To find the number of possible outfit combinations, multiply number of options for each factor:

$6 \times 4 \times 5 = 120$

**21) Choice C is correct**

Use simple interest formula: $I = prt$ $(I = interest, \ p = principal, \ r = rate, \ t = time)$

$I = (8,000)(0.045)(5) = 1,800$

**22) Choice C is correct**

Use percent formula: $\text{part} = \dfrac{\text{percent}}{100} \times \text{whole}$

$35 = \dfrac{percent}{100} \times 20 \Rightarrow 35 = \dfrac{percent \times 20}{100} \Rightarrow 35 = \dfrac{percent \times 2}{10}$, multiply both sides by 10.

$350 = percent \times 2$, divide both sides by 2.     $175 = percent$

**23) The answer is 260.**

The perimeter of the trapezoid is 64.

Therefore, the missing side (height) is $= 64 - 18 - 12 - 14 = 20$

Area of a trapezoid: $A = \frac{1}{2} h (b_1 + b_2) = \frac{1}{2} (20) (12 + 14) = 260$

**24) Choice C is correct**

Add the first 5 numbers. $46 + 45 + 50 + 35 + 55 = 231$. To find the distance traveled in the next 5 hours, multiply the average by number of hours. $Distance = Average \times Rate = 50 \times 5 = 250$,     Add both numbers. $250 + 231 = 481$

**25) Choice D is correct**

The equation of a line is in the form of $y = mx + b$, where $m$ is the slope of the line and $b$ is the $y - intercept$ of the line. Two points $(4,3)$ and $(3,2)$ are on line A. Therefore, the slope of the line A is: $slope \ of \ line \ A = \dfrac{y_2 - y_1}{x_2 - x_1} = \dfrac{2-3}{3-4} = \dfrac{-1}{-1} = 1$

The slope of line A is 1. Thus, the formula of the line A is: $y = mx + b = x + b$, choose a point and plug in the values of $x$ and $y$ in the equation to solve for $b$. Let's choose point $(4, 3)$. Then:

$y = x + b \rightarrow 3 = 4 + b \rightarrow b = 3 - 4 = -1$

The equation of line A is: $y = x - 1$

Now, let's review the choices provided:

A. $(-1, 2)$ $\qquad\qquad y = x - 1 \rightarrow 2 = -1 - 1 = -2 \qquad$ This is not true.

B. $(5, 7)$ $\qquad\qquad y = x - 1 \rightarrow 7 = 5 - 1 = 4 \qquad$ This is not true.

C. $(3, 4)$ $\qquad\qquad y = x - 1 \rightarrow 4 = 3 - 1 = 2 \qquad$ This is not true.

D. $(-1, -2)$ $\qquad\quad y = x - 1 \rightarrow -2 = -1 - 1 = -2 \quad$ This is true!

## 26) Choice C is correct

To find the discount, multiply the number by $(100\% - rate \ of \ discount)$.

Therefore, for the first discount we get: $(D) \ (100\% - 15\%) \ = \ (D) \ (0.85) \ = \ 0.85 \ D$

For increase of 10%: $(0.85 \ D) \ (100\% + 10\%) \ = \ (0.85 \ D) \ (1.10) \ = \ 0.93 \ D \ = \ 93\% \ of \ D$

## 27) Choice C is correct

Use distance formula: $C = \sqrt{(x_A - x_B)^2 + (y - y_B)^2} \rightarrow C = \sqrt{(1 - (-2))^2 + (3 - 7)^2} \rightarrow$

$$C = \sqrt{(3)^2 + (-4)^2} \rightarrow C = \sqrt{9 + 16} \rightarrow C = \sqrt{25} = 5$$

## 28) The answer is 200.

Th ratio of boy to girls is $2 : 3$. Therefore, there are 2 boys out of 5 students. To find the answer, first divide the total number of students by 5, then multiply the result by 2.

$500 \div 5 = 100 \Rightarrow 100 \times 2 = 200$

## 29) Choice B is correct

The question is this: 530.40 is what percent of 624?

Use percent formula: $part = \dfrac{percent}{100} \times whole$

$$530.40 = \frac{percent}{100} \times 624 \Rightarrow 530.40 = \frac{percent \times 624}{100} \Rightarrow 53040 = percent \times 624 \Rightarrow$$

$$percent = \frac{53040}{624} = 85$$

530.40 is 85% of 624. Therefore, the discount is: $100\% - 85\% = 15\%$

### 30) Choice D is correct

If 19 balls are removed from the bag at random, there will be one ball in the bag. The probability of choosing a brown ball is 1 out of 20. Therefore, the probability of not choosing a brown ball is 19 out of 20 and the probability of having not a brown ball after removing 19 balls is the same.

### 31) Choice C is correct

Let $x$ be the smallest number. Then, these are the numbers: $x, x + 1, x + 2, x + 3, x + 4$

average $= \frac{\text{sum of terms}}{\text{number of terms}} \Rightarrow 36 = \frac{x+(x+1)+(x+2)+(x+3)+(x+4)}{5} \Rightarrow 36 = \frac{5x+10}{5} \Rightarrow 180 = 5x + 10$
$\Rightarrow 170 = 5x \Rightarrow x = 34$

### 32) Choice C is correct

The weight of 14.2 meters of this rope is: $14.2 \times 600\ g = 8,520\ g$, $1\ kg = 1,000\ g$, therefore, $8,520\ g \div 1,000 = 8.52\ kg$

### 33) Choice B is correct

8% of the volume of the solution is alcohol. Let $x$ be the volume of the solution.

Then: $8\%\ of\ x = 38.4\ ml \Rightarrow 0.08\ x = 38.4 \Rightarrow x = 38.4 \div 0.08 = 480$

### 34) Choice D is correct

average $= \frac{\text{sum of terms}}{\text{number of terms}}$. The sum of the weight of all girls is: $18 \times 65 = 1,170\ kg$. The sum of the weight of all boys is: $32 \times 62 = 1,984\ kg$. The sum of the weight of all students is: $1,170 + 1,984 = 3,154\ kg$. $average = \frac{3,154}{50} = 63.08$

### 35) Choice B is correct

Write the numbers in order: $3, 5, 7, 8, 13, 15, 18$

Since we have 7 numbers (7 is odd), then the median is the number in the middle, which is 8

### 36) The answer is $533.8$

Surface Area of a cylinder $= 2\pi r\ (r + h)$,

The radius of the cylinder is 5 inches and its height is 12 inches. $\pi$ is 3.14. Then:

Surface Area of a cylinder $= 2\,(3.14)\,(5)\,(5+12)\ =\ 533.8$

**37) Choice A is correct**

Let $x$ be the number of years. Therefore, \$3,000 per year equals $3000x$.

starting from \$24,000 annual salary means you should add that amount to $3000x$.

Income more than that is: $I > 3,000x\ + 24,000$

**38) Choice B is correct**

The question is this: 1.75 is what percent of 1.40? Use percent formula:

$$\text{part}\ =\frac{\text{percent}}{100}\times\text{whole} \Rightarrow 1.75 =\frac{percent}{100}\times 1.40\ \Rightarrow\ 1.75 =\frac{percent\ \times 1.40}{100}$$

$$\Rightarrow 175 =\ percent\ \times 1.40\ \Rightarrow\ percent\ =\frac{1.75}{1.40} =\ 125$$

**39) Choice B is correct**

Use the information provided in the question to draw the shape.

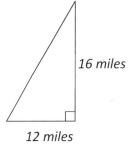

16 miles

12 miles

Use Pythagorean Theorem: $a^2 + b^2 = c^2$

$12^2 + 16^2 = c^2 \Rightarrow 144 + 256 = c^2 \Rightarrow 400 = c^2 \Rightarrow c = 20$

**40) Choice A is correct**

For each option, choose a point in the solution part and check it on both inequalities.

$y \leq x + 4$
$2x + y \leq -4$

    A.  Point $(-4, -4)$ is in the solution section. Let's check the point in both inequalities.

$-4\ \leq\ -4\ +\ 4$, It works

$2\,(-4) + (-4) \leq -4 \Rightarrow\ -12\ \leq\ -4$, it works (this point works in both inequalities)

    B.  Let's choose this point $(0, 0)$
        $0\ \leq\ 0\ +\ 4$, It works
        $2\,(0) +\ (0) \leq -4$, That's not true!

    C.  Let's choose this point $(-5, 0)$
        $0\ \leq -5\ +\ 4$, That's not true!

    D.  Let's choose this point $(0, 5)$
        $5\ \leq 0\ +\ 4$, That's not true!

Only choice A represents both inequalities.

# STAAR Mathematics Practice Test 5

## Answers and Explanations

**1) Choice C is correct**

$4x - 2y = 2x$ has a graph that is a straight line. All other options are not equations of straight lines.

**2) Choice D is correct.**

When a point is reflected over $x$ axes, the $(y)$ coordinate of that point changes to $(-y)$ while its $x$ coordinate remains the same. C $(7, 9) \rightarrow$ C' $(7, -9)$

**3) The correct answer is 12**

Use the volume of the triangular prism formula.

V = $\frac{1}{2}$ (length) (base) (high)

V = $\frac{1}{2} \times 4 \times 3 \times 2 \Rightarrow$ V = 12 m$^3$

**4) Choice A is correct**

$2x + 4 > 11x - 12.5 - 3.5x \rightarrow$ Combine like terms: $2x + 4 > 7.5x - 12.5 \rightarrow$ Subtract $2x$ from both sides: $4 > 5.5x - 12.5$. Add 12.5 both sides of the inequality. $16.5 > 5.5x$, Divide both sides by 5.5. $\frac{16.5}{5.5} > x \rightarrow x < 3$

**5) Choice D is correct**

$3x - 5 = 8.5 \rightarrow 3x = 8.5 + 5 = 13.5 \rightarrow x = \frac{13.5}{3} = 4.5$

Then; $6x + 3 = 6 (4.5) + 3 = 27 + 3 = 30$

**6) Choice D is correct**

First draw an isosceles triangle. Remember that two sides of the triangle are equal.

Let put $a$ for the legs. Then:

Isosceles right triangle

$a = 8 \Rightarrow$ area of the triangle is $= \frac{1}{2}(8 \times 8) = \frac{64}{2} = 32 \ cm^2$

**7) Choice D is correct**

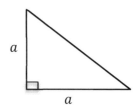

To find the discount, multiply the number by $(100\% - rate\ of\ discount)$.

Therefore, for the first discount we get: $(600)\ (100\% - 25\%) = (600)\ (0.75)$

For the next 15% discount: $(600)(0.75)(0.85)$

**8) Choice A is correct**

Plug in each pair of numbers in the equation: $3x + 5y = 11$

    A. $(2, 1)$:          $3\ (2) + 5\ (1) = 11$
    B. $(-1, 2)$:       $3\ (-1) + 5\ (2) = 7$
    C. $(-2, 2)$:       $3\ (-2) + 5\ (2) = 4$
    D. $(2, 2)$:          $3\ (2) + 5\ (2) = 16$

Choice A is correct.

**9) The answer is$-3$.**

Use PEMDAS (order of operation): $-15 + 6 \times (-5) - [4 + 22 \times (-4)] \div 2 =$

$$-15 - 30 - [4 - 88] \div 2 = -45 - [-84] \div 2 = -45 + 84 \div 2 = -45 + 42 = -3$$

**10) Choice B is correct**

6% of the volume of the solution is alcohol. Let $x$ be the volume of the solution.

Then: $6\%\ of\ x = 24\ ml \Rightarrow 0.06\ x = 24 \Rightarrow x = 24 \div 0.06 = 400$

**11) Choice B is correct**

$$average\ = \frac{\text{sum of terms}}{\text{number of terms}}$$

The sum of the weight of all girls is: $18 \times 60 = 1080\ kg$, The sum of the weight of all boys is: $32 \times 62 = 1984\ kg$, The sum of the weight of all students is: $1080 + 1984 = 3064\ kg$

$$average\ = \frac{3064}{50} = 61.28$$

**12) The answer is $1, 205. 76$**

Surface Area of a cylinder $= 2\pi r\ (r + h)$,

The radius of the cylinder is 8 inches and its height is 12 inches. $\pi$ is 3.14. Then:

Surface Area of a cylinder $= 2\ (3.14)\ (8)\ (8 + 16) = 1205.76$

**13) Choice A is correct**

Let $x$ be the number of years. Therefore, $\$2,000\ per\ year$ equals $2000x$. starting from $27,000 annual salary means you should add that amount to $2000x$.

Income more than that is: $I > 2000x + 27000$

**14) The answer is 5.**

Solving Systems of Equations by Elimination

$3x - 4y = -20$
$\underline{-x + 2y = 10}$    Multiply the second equation by 3, then add it to the first equation.

$\begin{array}{c} 3x - 4y = -20 \\ \underline{3(-x + 2y = 10)} \end{array} \Rightarrow \begin{array}{c} 3x - 4y = -20 \\ \underline{-3x + 6y = 30} \end{array} \Rightarrow 2y = 10 \Rightarrow y = 5$

**15) Choice B is correct**

The diagonal of the square is 6 meters. Let $x$ be the side.
Use Pythagorean Theorem: $a^2 + b^2 = c^2$
$x^2 + x^2 = 6^2 \Rightarrow 2x^2 = 6^2 \Rightarrow 2x^2 = 36 \Rightarrow x^2 = 18 \Rightarrow x = \sqrt{18}$
The area of the square is: $\sqrt{18} \times \sqrt{18} = 18\ m^2$

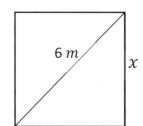

**16) Choice D is correct**

If the length of the box is 24, then the width of the box is one third of it, 8, and the height of the box is 4 (half of the width). The volume of the box is: $V = lwh = (24)(8)(4) = 768$

**17) Choice D is correct**

Write the equation and solve for B: $0.60A = 0.20B$, divide both sides by 0.20, then:

$\frac{0.60}{0.20}A = B$, therefore: $B = 3A$, and B is 3 times of $A$ or it's 300% of $A$.

**18) Choice C is correct**

Use simple interest formula: $I = prt\ (I = interest,\ p = principal,\ r = rate,\ t = time)$

$I = (8,000)(0.025)(5) = 1,000$

**19) The answer is 78.**

The perimeter of the trapezoid is 50. Therefore, the missing side (height) is $= 50 - 18 - 12 - 14 = 6$, Area of a trapezoid: $A = \frac{1}{2}h(b_1 + b_2) = \frac{1}{2}(6)(12 + 14) = 78$

**20) Choice B is correct**

Add the first 5 numbers. $40 + 45 + 50 + 35 + 55 = 225$

To find the distance traveled in the next 5 hours, multiply the average by number of hours.

Distance = Average × Rate = $45 \times 5 = 225$,    Add both numbers. $225 + 225 = 450$

**21) Choice D is correct.**

Plug in each pair of numbers in the equation. The answer should be 20.

A. $(2, 1)$:     $4(2) + 6(1) = 14$     No!
B. $(-1, 3)$:     $4(-1) + 6(2) = 8$     No!
C. $(-2, 2)$:     $4(-2) + 6(2) = 4$     No!
D. $(2, 2)$:     $4(2) + 6(2) = 20$     Yes!

**22) Choice C is correct**

Let $x$ be the number. Write the equation and solve for $x$.

$\frac{2}{3} \times 15 = \frac{2}{5} \cdot x \Rightarrow \frac{2 \times 15}{3} = \frac{2x}{5}$ , use cross multiplication to solve for $x$. $5 \times 30 = 2x \times 3 \Rightarrow$

$150 = 6x \Rightarrow x = 25$

**23) Choice C is correct**

To find the discount, multiply the number by $(100\% - rate\ of\ discount)$.

Therefore, for the first discount we get: $(D)(100\% - 20\%) = (D)(0.80) = 0.80\ D$

For increase of 15%: $(0.80D)(100\% + 15\%) = (0.80\ D)(1.15) = 0.92\ D = 92\%\ of\ D$

**24) Choice B is correct**

Use the formula for Percent of Change: $\frac{New\ Value - Old\ Value}{Old\ Value} \times 100\%$

$\frac{28 - 4}{45} \times 100\% = -37.7\%$ (negative sign here means that the new price is less than old price).

**25) Choice D is correct**

Some of prime numbers are: $2, 3, 5, 7, 11, 13$. Find the product of two consecutive prime numbers: $2 \times 3 = 6$ (not in the options), $3 \times 5 = 15$ (bingo!), $5 \times 7 = 35$ (yes!) ,$7 \times 11 = 77$ (not in the options). Choice D is correct.

**26) The answer is 160.**

Th ratio of boy to girls is $2 : 3$. Therefore, there are 2 boys out of 5 students. To find the answer, first divide the total number of students by 5, then multiply the result by 2. $400 \div 5 = 80 \Rightarrow 80 \times 2 = 160$

**27) Choice B is correct**

The question is this: 530.40 is what percent of 631? Use percent formula:

$part = \frac{percent}{100} \times whole$ , $530.40 = \frac{percent}{100} \times 6331 \Rightarrow 530.40 = \frac{percent \times 631}{100} \Rightarrow$

$530.40 = percent \times 631 \Rightarrow percent = \frac{530.40}{631} = 84.05 \cong 84$

530.40 is 84% of 631. Therefore, the discount is: $100\% - 84\% = 16\%$

**28) Choice B is correct**

If the score of Mia was 60, therefore the score of Ava is 30. Since, the score of Emma was half as that of Ava, therefore, the score of Emma is 15.

**29) Choice D is correct**

If 20 balls are removed from the bag at random, there will be one ball in the bag. The probability of choosing a white ball is 1 out of 21. Therefore, the probability of not choosing a white ball is 20 out of 21 and the probability of having not a white ball after removing 20 balls is the same.

**30) The answer is 52.**

$$\text{average} = \frac{\text{sum of terms}}{\text{number of terms}} \Rightarrow 25 = \frac{13+15+20+}{4} \Rightarrow 100 = 48 + x \Rightarrow x = 52$$

**31) Choice C is correct**

The sum of supplement angles is 180. Let $x$ be that angle. Therefore, $x + 4x = 180$

$5x = 180$, divide both sides by 5: $x = 36$

**32) Choice C is correct**

Use Pythagorean Theorem: $a^2 + b^2 = c^2$

$5^2 + 12^2 = c^2 \Rightarrow 25 + 144 = c^2 \Rightarrow 169 = c^2 \Rightarrow c = 13$

**33) Choice A is correct**

Area of the circle is less than $14\,\pi$. Use the formula of areas of circles.

$$Area = \pi r^2 \Rightarrow 49\,\pi > \pi r^2 \Rightarrow 49 > r^2 \Rightarrow r < 7$$

Radius of the circle is less than 7. Let's put 7 for the radius. Now, use the circumference formula: $Circumference = 2\pi r = 2\pi\,(7) = 14\pi$. Since the radius of the circle is less than 7. Then, the circumference of the circle must be less than $14\pi$. Only choice A is less than $14\pi$.

**34) Choice D is correct**

Simplify the inequality: $2y + 6 < 30 \rightarrow 2y < 30 - 6 \rightarrow 2y < 24 \rightarrow y < 12$. Only choice D (8) is less than 12.

**35) Choice C is correct**

The question is this: 185.00 is what percent of 125.00? Use percent formula:

$\frac{185}{125} = 1.48$ or $148\%$

**36) Choice B is correct**

Use the information provided in the question to draw the shape.

Use Pythagorean Theorem: $\quad a^2 + b^2 = c^2$

$80^2 + 150^2 = c^2 \Rightarrow 6{,}400 + 22{,}500 = c^2 \Rightarrow 28{,}900 = c^2 \Rightarrow c = 170$

$80 \ miles$

$150 \ miles$

**37) Choice C is correct.**

A graph represents $y$ as a function of $x$ if

$x_1 = x_2 \rightarrow y_1 = y_2$

In choice C, for each $x$, we have two different values for $y$.

**38) Choice A is correct**

$13 < -3x - 2 < 22 \rightarrow$ Add 2 to all sides. $13 + 2 < -3x - 2 + 2 < 22 + 2$

$\rightarrow 15 < -3x < 24 \rightarrow$ Divide all sides by $-3$. (Remember that when you divide all sides of an inequality by a negative number, the inequality sing will be swapped. < becomes >)

$\dfrac{15}{-3} > \dfrac{-3x}{-3} > \dfrac{24}{-3}.$ $\qquad -8 < x < -5$

**39) Choice B is correct**

Number of biology book: 35. Total number of books; $35 + 95 + 80 = 210$

The ratio of the number of biology books to the total number of books is: $\dfrac{35}{210} = \dfrac{1}{6}$

**40) Choice C is correct**

$\begin{cases} 5x + y = 9 \\ 10x - 7y = -18 \end{cases} \Rightarrow$ Multiply (–2) to the first equation $\Rightarrow \begin{cases} -10x - 2y = -18 \\ 10x - 7y = -18 \end{cases}$

Add two equations $\Rightarrow -9y = -36 \Rightarrow y = 4$, plugin the value of $y$ in the first equation and solve for $x$. Then: $-10x - 2y = -18 \Rightarrow -10x - 2(4) = -18 \Rightarrow -10x - 8 = -18$. Add 8 to both sides. Then: $-10x - 8 + 8 = -18 + 8 \Rightarrow -10x = -10 \Rightarrow x = 1$

Only in choice C (1, 4) the value of $x$ is 1.

## "Effortless Math Education" Publications

Effortless Math authors' team strives to prepare and publish the best quality STAAR Mathematics learning resources to make learning Math easier for all. We hope that our publications help you learn Math in an effective way and prepare for the STAAR test.

We all in Effortless Math wish you good luck and successful studies!

Effortless Math Authors

# www.EffortlessMath.com

... So Much More Online!

✓ FREE Math lessons

✓ More Math learning books!

✓ Mathematics Worksheets

✓ Online Math Tutors

**Need a PDF version of this book?**

Visit www.EffortlessMath.com

Made in the USA
Coppell, TX
23 June 2022

79166663R00057